How ^{NOT} to Write a Screenplay

a Screenplay

101 Common Mistakes Most Screenwriters Make

Denny Martin Flinn

ifilm publishing   lone eagle

HOW *NOT* TO WRITE A SCREENPLAY
101 Common Mistakes Most Screenwriters Make
Copyright © 1999 by Denny Martin Flinn

LONE EAGLE PUBLISHING COMPANY™
1024 North Orange Drive
Hollywood, California 90038
Phone 323.308.3400 or 800.815.0503
A division of IFILM® Corp., www.ifilm.com

Printed in the United States of America

Cover design by Lindsay Albert
Book design by Carla Green
Edited by Lauren Rossini

Library of Congress Cataloging-in-Publication Data

Flinn, Denny Martin.
     How not to write a screenplay : 101 common mistakes most screenwriters make / Denny Martin Flinn.
        p.   cm.
     ISBN 1-58065-015-5
     1. Motion picture authorship. 2 Television authorship.
3. Motion picture plays—Technique. 4. Television plays—Technique.
I. Title.
PN1996.F46 1999
808.2'3—dc21   99-33128
                                              CIP

Books may be purchased in bulk at special discounts for promotional or educational purposes. Special editions can be created to specifications. Inquiries for sales and distribution, textbook adoption, foreign language translation, editorial, and rights and permissions inquiries should be addressed to: Jeff Black, IFILM Publishing, 1024 North Orange Drive, Hollywood, California 90038 or send e-mail to: info@ifilm.com

Distributed to the trade by National Book Network, 800.462.6420

IFILM is a registered trademark.
Lone Eagle Publishing Company is a registered trademark.

No man but a blockhead
ever wrote except for
money.

Samuel Johnson
(1709-1784)

CONTENTS

Acknowledgments

Thanks to...
my wife Barbara, who is, in writing and life, my front line editor,
Deborah Schneider, my unreasonably loyal agent,
Nicholas Meyer and Bernard Sofronski, who arranged for me to read all those awful scripts,
Greg Boone, for legal advice,
and Scott Benton, for the best development notes in the business.

Excerpts from *The Abyss* © Twentieth Century Fox Film Corporation 1989

Excerpts from *The Adventures of Buckaroo Banzai Across the Eighth Dimension* © Sherwood Productions Inc. 1984

Excerpts from *Alien* © Twentieth-Century Fox Film Corporation 1979

Excerpts from *Aliens* © Twentieth-Century Fox Film Corporation 1986

Excerpt from *Aliens vs. Predator* © Peter Briggs

Excerpt from *Annie Hall* © United Artists Corporation 1977

Excerpt from *Becket* © Paramount 1964

Excerpts from *Blade Runner* © Warner Bros. 1982

Excerpts from *Braveheart* © B.H. Finance C.V. 1995

Excerpt from *Casablanca* © Warner Bros. Pictures 1943

Excerpt from *The Crying Game* © Palace (Soldier's Wife), Ltd., & Nippon Film Development and Finance, Inc. 1992

Excerpt from *Die Hard* © Twentieth Century Fox Film Corporation 1988

Excerpt from *Don Q* © Nicholas Meyer

Excerpt from *The Usual Suspects* © Rosco Film, GmbH, & Bad Hat Harry Productions, Ltd. 1995

Excerpt from *When Harry Met Sally* © Castle Rock Entertainment 1989

Excerpt from *White Heat* © Warner Bros. 1949

Quotation from the *American Heritage Dictionary* © Houghton Mifflin Company 1982

Quotation from *Monster, Living off the Big Screen* © John Gregory Dunne 1998

Quotations from Aristotles' *Poetics* translation © Thomas Y. Crowell Company, Inc. 1969

Quotation from Goethe translation © Thomas Y. Crowell Company, Inc. 1969

Quotation from "Trouble Is My Business" © Raymond Chandler 1939

Les Trente-Six Situations Dramatique by Georges Polti, published Boston: The Writer Inc. 1977, translation by Lucille Ray

Form and Meaning in Fiction by Norman Friedman, published University of Georgia Press 1975

INTRODUCTION

The first thing you really want to know when you're buying a book about screenwriting is. . .who is this guy? Has he won an Oscar?

(No. A few years ago I shared a nomination for "best adaptation for a radio drama" from the British Writer's Guild, but I couldn't afford to go over for the dinner.)

Has he written any great movies?

(No. My only produced credit to date is *Star Trek VI: The Undiscovered Country*.)

So, why should you buy my book?

I didn't write this because I can write screenplays. I wrote this because I have had to read tons of them. I came to understand that while all good screenplays are unique, all bad screenplays are the same. I am amazed at how often this is confirmed for me in a new, bad screenplay. It occurred to me that there are screenwriters out there who might like to hear from their principal audience— the reader.

I think a novel takes more raw talent than technique, but a screenplay takes more technique. A screenplay is like a crossword puzzle. Not only do you need the right word, you need the word with the right number of letters. Screenplays are not literature. Nobody reads screenplays for fun, believe me. Reading screenplays is done by people who are looking for one to turn into a movie. These people *love* to make movies and *hate* to read.

But they have to read screenplays to find movies to make. So these people have to read a lot of screenplays when they would much rather be out making movies, making deals, and doing lunch.

What these people read a lot of is bad screenplays, because 35,707 were registered last year with the Writer's Guild of America, about 99 percent of which are terrible. If there is one thing they can spot quickly, it's a bad screenplay. (They are so used to bad screenplays, they tend to forget what good ones are like, and they lie awake nights in the fear that they'll miss The One.)

If your screenplay gives them any indication it will be one of those bad screenplays, they're going to spot it right off and then it's all uphill. If your reader is actually a producer, director, star, studio executive or agent, they are more likely to skip to the end as soon as they've made an evaluation. If you've got a reader forced to slog through the whole thing because they have to write "coverage" (a Hollywood book report), they will read through to the bitter end, then send a scathing criticism of your life's work to their boss. (As the producer says to the writer in the Broadway musical *City of Angels*, "I've read coverage on every thing you've ever written!")

Even if they read your screenplay all the way through, the big question is, are they going to want to make your film? Do they believe anyone will want to see it? While scintillating prose can make reading your screenplay a pleasure, what you are really writing is a *blueprint for a film.*

You've probably thumbed through half a dozen books on screenwriting already, and what you really want to know is, is this the one that will teach me to write a good screenplay?

No. This book is not going to teach you good writing. If you're a writer, you will develop your own ideas and your own style, and no one should talk you out of that. This book is going to teach you how to avoid the pitfalls of bad screenwriting, and arrive at your own destination intact.

I have collected a plethora of faults that, over the pages, I have come to recognize as all too common. Every example used here was gleaned from a legitimate screenplay. (Nouns have been changed to protect the inept.) These are things that have made me want to shout, *"That's a dumb mistake!"* This is my chance.

If you can avoid the faults I have collected here, you may not write a particularly good screenplay. But you won't write a bad one. The rest is up to you.

I've divided the book into two parts, form and content. (All art can be divided into form and content, why not screenplays?) Some of what follows may seem ridiculously obvious, but I've included everything because—I swear—I have seen each of these errors more than once in supposedly bona fide, agency-submitted screenplays.

Part 1

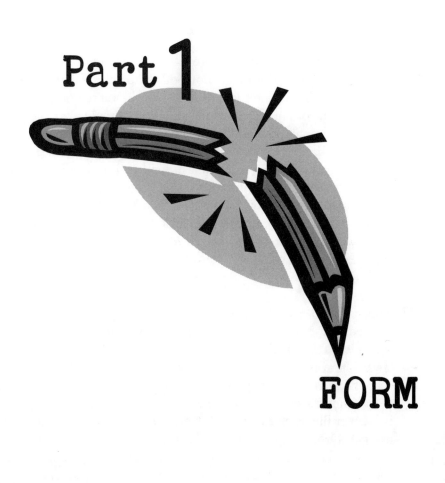

FORM

Put your name, address, and phone number on the title page.

You would be amazed how many screenplays have no contact information at all on the manuscript itself. If you do not want direct calls (you should be so lucky), at least make sure your agency is listed on the title page, along with their address and phone number.

Information on cover letters does not count. Your correspondence with producers is lost at a rate close to 100 percent. Even if you give a script to your best friend, you have no idea who may end up reading it down the road.

However, do not expect more than a 10 percent return rate at best. Most people simply do not bother to return manuscripts. (Pretty rude, but in the rudeness category, if you're going to be a screenwriter, you ain't seen nothin' yet.) If they should like it, they've got to get in touch with you. If they aren't interested in the screenplay per se, but like your writing (*all* scripts are sample scripts in that sense, and you never know who will end up reading it who might be looking for a writer for another project) they have to know *how to contact you.* Easily. Try to keep it current. They have a very limited patience with tracking people down. I'm afraid that's part of the out-of-sight, out-of-mind syndrome which plays such a big part in the Hollywood game.

Titles

There is some confusion over whether or not titles are copyrightable. Here's the McCoy: they are not included in Federal copyright laws. There are two exceptions, however.

One, if a title is a registered trademark, such as *Nestle's Crunch*, or has an intrinsic value (because it has been hugely successful and is identifiable) such as *Gone With the Wind*, you could be sued for using it. Or for stupidity.

Two, there is a Hollywood title registration program as part of the Motion Picture Association of America, to which all major studios and many independents belong. This means they can register a feature film title—*even if they currently have no film or screenplay by that name*—and other members of the association agree not to use it. You would be surprised how many titles are registered, simply in the hope that they will one day prove useful.

Do your homework. I once enthusiastically picked up a screenplay entitled *Dark of the Moon*, in the expectation that someone had done a film adaptation of that famous, classic folk play, only to read a third rate horror film. *The Rainmaker* is a famous play by N. Richard Nash (the film version start Burt Lancaster and Katharine Hepburn) and no John Grisham novel should ever eclipse it.

Generic titles are very popular these days. But bear in mind that someone else out there is calling his script the same thing. In the last few years, I've read half a dozen spec scripts titled "Clean Sweep," and at least a dozen titled "Dead Wrong." Better to try to come up with a unique title. (It might not help. Disney changed "In the Hall of the Mountain King" to *Shoot to Kill*.) Why generic titles are so popular is beyond me, since they neither jump out at you, nor give you an impression of their content, two virtues which advertising experts advise. Yet in a recent visit to a video store, I noticed the shelves groaning with titles like. . .

Above Suspicion	Deep Cover	Maximum Risk
Above the Law	Extreme Measures	New York Cop
Beyond Justice	Extreme Justice	Out for Justice
Boiling Point	Extreme Prejudice	Physical Evidence
Code of Silence	Fair Game	Serial Killer
Cop	Fatal Error	Sudden Impact
D.O.A.	Fatal Attraction	Sudden Death
Dead Again	Hard to Kill	Super Cop
Dead to Rights	Hard Evidence	Time to Die
Dead Ringers	Homicide	Time to Kill
Dead of Winter	Lethal Weapon	True Crime
Dead Calm	Magnum Force	Under Investigation
Dead Center	Maniac Cop	Under Suspicion
Deadly Outbreak	Marked for Death	Unlawful Entry
Deadly Surveillance	Martial Law	etc.

I worked on a film that needed a new title in post-production because the working title was taken. We got a list of suggestions from the studio's marketing department, and it read almost exactly like the above.

In other words, there is no good or bad advice about titles, because there are no good or bad titles. (A good title, it's been said, is the title of a success.) If you've got a good movie, everyone will remember your title. If you don't, even a title as unique as *Ishtar* won't help.

Sub-titles

Most screenplays shouldn't have one. For example: "A Romantic Comedy." We'll be the judge of that.

Written by (your credit)

Here are a few official definitions (from the Writer's Guild) to bear in mind:

Written by means that the same person or team wrote both the story and the screenplay.

Story by means that the writer or writers devised not only the situation and characters but the basic sequence of action in the film.

Screenplay by means that the writer or writers created the dialogue and probably made some significant contributions to the development.

Screen story by means that the writer relied on a book, play or other source material, but so thoroughly reworked it that he is acknowledged for having created something new.

Adaptation by is a very rare credit, used "to mean something that it never otherwise means in the English language." It covers an instance in which a writer has neither created the story nor written the bulk of the dialogue, but has made some fundamental change in the material.

Narration by, an even more rare credit, is given when the voice-over narration of a film amounts to a dominant voice, as in *Never Cry Wolf*, or *Apocalypse Now*.

An ampersand (&) between names designates them as a writing team, while "and" between the names means they worked independently.

If you are rewriting someone else's script, the W.G.A. requires the following title page format:

1. Name of Project by (name of first writer)
2. Based on (source material, if any) by (name of author)

3. Revisions by (names of subsequent writers in order of work performed)

4. Current revisions by (current writer, date)

In any case, when a film gets made, the screenwriting credit won't be up to you, the producer, or even the studio. It's up to the Guild, so for now you can simply put "by" and keep your dues current.

Copyright

You can copyright your screenplay if you want to. Get Form PA from the Register of Copyrights, Copyright Office, Library of Congress, Washington D.C. 20559-6000, and return it with your screenplay and $20.00.

The Writers Guild of America, West has a registration program conducted out of their offices at 7000 West Third Street, Los Angeles, CA 90038. The WGA East has a separate one—555 West 57th Street, New York, New York 10019. (They're both online as well.) For a nominal fee, you give them the script and they keep it, dated. The WGA doesn't give legal advice, testify, or back one writer over another. But if a lawsuit or arbitration ever arises, they can authenticate the date of origin. You needn't be a member of the union to utilize this service.

Copyright or registration isn't necessary, however. Current copyright law basically states that if it comes out of your typewriter, it's yours. Registration merely establishes what you wrote when.

If you are convinced somebody stole your screenplay and you are going to take them to court, it will be incumbent upon you to establish when you wrote it. Either of these programs will do that. Mailing the script to yourself, or photographing yourself holding it and a dated newspaper at the same time, are two old dime novel devices, but the judge may not be familiar with film noir and may not be amused. In fact, all you have to do is show it to a few reliable friends. Even your spouse, if you can stand the criticism.

Don't, however, **put a copyright or registration notice on the title page.** There is no need for this, and it smacks of amateurism. You'll see it on the title page when a studio buys it. "Property Of" will be stamped all over it. And your "copyright" is kaput.

Don't write "First Draft" on your title page.

This depresses a reader before he even opens to FADE IN. If it's your first—or any other—*draft*, keep working and leave us alone.

The exception is writing on assignment. If they have to pay you for turning in a "first draft," then again for turning in a "second draft," give them a hint it's pay day.

However, you should always put a date on the title page. Dates become necessary when subsequent drafts start to pile up. Every author has received a call from his agent's secretary—usually late Friday afternoon—asking which draft is the most recent because Spielberg wants to read it over the weekend. This can also date your script; when a producer sees that a manuscript he has scooped up is two years old, he tends to wonder why no one has bought it yet. So keep the date as current as you can.

Don't put the name of a production company on your screenplay, unless it has been purchased.

Do not make up a name for your own non-existent production company. Authors apparently do this in the mistaken belief it makes them sound important. You and your friend who hope to make a film one day are not a production company. An unattached screenplay is far more interesting than one with attachments that are not bankable.

Do not include synopsis, photographs, reviews or coverage with your screenplay.

A synopsis plays right into the reader's hands. He won't have to read your screenplay. Photos, like art work, don't help. They limit the reader's imagination rather than encourage it. Good coverage you may have gotten from an earlier reader only leads the current reader to say to himself, "Oh yeah? We'll see. . ."

This goes for your cover letter as well. **Don't rave about your own screenplay.** "You'll find it riveting and dramatic." We'll be the judge. **Don't cast it.** "I see Tom Cruise in the lead." Who doesn't? Let the reader use his own imagination in casting. **Don't tell us how commercial it is.** Everyone thinks their screenplay is commercial, though very few are.

My least favorite cover letter runs:

```
Dear Sir:

    Here is my screenplay HEARTS AFIRE. It's
warmhearted and adult, yet very commercial.
Loaded with action and comedy, it's really a
serious drama about the intense relationship
of two real people. The role of Bill is
perfect for Dustin Hoffman, and the role of
Sally would be ideal for Meryl Streep, Jane
Fonda or Barbara Streisand. It is very low
budget, yet is a potentially large-grossing
film.

    I will call you next week to discuss it
further.

Yours sincerely,

Starving Writer
```

A simple, "as per our conversation, enclosed you will find," along with a "thanks for taking a look. . ." will be enough.

Don't list a cast of characters.

That's correct for a play or an episode of a continuing television series. For a feature film or television film screenplay, let each new character come to us the way it will on screen.

Margins

There is no exact rule on these. Most software programs for screenwriting have standard templates, but they vary and generally you'll want to set your own. Going by standard columns, at ten character columns per inch, a good looking, well-spaced screenplay will run something like this:

- SLUGLINES (capitalized):

Column 15, or 1 and 1/2 inches in. This seems like a fairly wide left-hand margin, but when more than 100 pages are bound, you'll need it. Don't force the reader to go digging for the first word on every line.

- Action description:

The same, not capitalized.

- CHARACTER NAMES (capitalized):

Begin at column 35 (3 1/2" from left edge). **Don't center them.** They should all start at the same column.

Wrong:

                    PINCUS
          Damn!

                    BECKWITH
          You're losing your
          concentration.

                    HELEN
          It's that case. He's always
          thinking about it.

                    BECKWITH
          He's with you every minute?

Right:

               BECKET
          Tonight you can do me the
          honor of christening my
          forks.

               KING HENRY
          Forks?

               BECKET
          Yes, from Florence. New
          little invention. It's for
          pronging meat and carrying
          it to the mouth. It saves
          you dirtying your fingers.

```
          KING HENRY
But then you dirty the fork.

          BECKET
Yes, but it's washable.

          KING HENRY
So are your fingers. I don't
see the point.¹
```

• (Parenthetical phrases):

Hints to the actor should run between columns 30 (3") and 50 or 55 (5"—5-1/2"). Hints in the middle of a speech can flow along with the dialogue (in parentheses) or, if you want to give the hint

(more weight),

can have a line of their own.

• Dialogue:

A left hand margin of 25 (2-1/2") to a right hand margin of 55 (5-1/2"), with a wrap tolerance of four to six letters. This is your most flexible definition. I've seen smart looking screenplays with a dialogue column of anywhere between two and a half and four and a half inches wide. **Don't hyphenate dialogue.**

• TRANSITIONS (capitalized):

Start at column 55 (5 1/2" from left edge). Some writers line up the right hand column (right justification):

```
                                        CUT TO:

                                    DISSOLVE TO:

                                        WIPE TO:
```

but it looks neater to line up the left side:

```
                         CUT TO:

                         DISSOLVE TO:

                         WIPE TO:
```

• Right hand margin:

Column 75, leaving a right hand margin of 1", with a wrap tolerance of four to six letters.

In other words:

```
                                                            1.


inches:
1.5"        2.5"3"     3.5"              5"    5.5"              7.5"

columns:
15          25   30    35                50    55



SCENE SLUGLINE

Action, description  ────────────────────────────────────


                    CHARACTER NAME
                 (parenthetical phrase)
                 Dialogue goes here and is
                 neither hyphenated or
                 right-justified.

                                TRANSITION:


NEW SCENE
```

• Single space *within* paragraphs of action description, dialogue, and between a character's name and his or her dialogue. Double space *between* these paragraphs. Some formats utilize triple-spacing between scenes, as in:

```
She hurries out the door, her limp impeding her
slightly.


INT. SECOND FLOOR HALLWAY - DAY
```

But this is a lot of wasted space. Double space between scenes:

<pre>
                    TOMBS
          Don't look round. Slip
          quietly out, old man. It's
          the Brigadier.

They leave with the utmost caution.

INT. SACHER'S RECEPTION HALL - DAY ²
</pre>

Now let's look at a few pages of properly formatted writing:

<pre>
                                                 1.

INT. TYRELL CORPORATION LOCKER ROOM - DAY

THE EYE

It's magnified and deeply revealed. Flecks of green
and yellow in a field of milky blue. Icy filaments
surround the undulating center.

The eye is shown in a tiny screen. On the metallic
surface below, the words VOIGHT-KAMPFF are finely
etched. There's a touch-light panel across the top
and on the side of the screen, a dial that
registers fluctuations of the iris.

The instrument is no bigger than a music box and
sits on a table between two men. The man talking is
big, looks like an overstuffed kid. "LEON" it says
on his breast pocket. He's dressed in a
warehouseman's uniform and his pudgy hands are
folded expectantly in his lap. Despite the obvious
heat, he looks very cool.

The man facing him is lean, hollow cheeked and
dressed in gray. Detached and efficient, he looks
like a cop or an accountant. His name is HOLDEN and
he's all business, except for the sweat on his
face.
</pre>

The room is large and humid. Rows of salvaged junk
are stacked neatly against the walls. Two large
fans whir above their heads.

> LEON
> Okay if I talk?

Holden doesn't answer. He's centering Leon's eye on
the machine.

> LEON
> I kinda get nervous when I
> take tests.

> HOLDEN
> Don't move.

> LEON
> Sorry.

He tries not to move but finally his lips can't
help a sheepish smile.

> LEON
> Already had I.Q. test this
> year—but I don't think I
> never had a...

> HOLDEN
> (cutting in)
> Reaction time is a factor in
> this, so please pay
> attention. Answer quickly as
> you can.

Leon compresses his lips and nods his big head
eagerly. Holden's voice is cold, geared to
intimidate and evoke response.

> HOLDEN
> You're in a desert, walking
> along in the sand when all
> of a sudden you look down
> and see a...

> LEON
> What one?

It was a timid interruption, hardly audible.

> HOLDEN
> What?

> LEON
> What desert?

> HOLDEN
> Doesn't make any difference
> what desert—it's completely
> hypothetical.

> LEON
> But how come I'd be there?

> HOLDEN
> Maybe you're fed up, maybe
> you want to be by yourself—
> who knows. So you look down
> and see a tortoise. It's
> crawling towards you...

> LEON
> A tortoise. What's that?

> HOLDEN
> Know what a turtle is?

> LEON
> Of course.

> HOLDEN
> Same thing.

> LEON
> I never seen a turtle.

He sees Holden's patience is wearing thin.

              LEON
But I understand what you
mean.

            HOLDEN
You reach down and flip the
tortoise over on its back,
Leon.

Keeping an eye on his subject, Holden notes the
dials in the Voight-Kampff. One of the needles
quivers slightly.

             LEON
You make these questions,
Mr. Holden, or they write
'em down for you?

Disregarding the question, Holden continues,
picking up the pace.

            HOLDEN
The tortoise lays on its
back, its belly baking in
the hot sun, beating its
legs trying to turn itself
over. But it can't. Not
without your help. But
you're not helping.

Leon's upper lip is quivering.

             LEON
Whatcha mean, I'm not
helping?

            HOLDEN
I mean you're not helping!
Why is that, Leon?

Leon looks shocked, surprised. But the needles in
the computer barely move. Holden goes for the
inside of his coat. But big Leon is faster. His
LASER BURNS a hole the size of a nickel through
Holden's stomach. Unlike a bullet, a laser causes

no impact. It goes through Holden's spine and comes
out his back, clean as a whistle. Like a rag doll
he falls back off the bench from the waist up. [3]

A recently popular way to format action is a series of terse lines, each starting at the margin. It has the virtue of a fast, staccato rhythm not unlike a salesman jabbing you in the chest to make his point. Used cautiously, it has its uses:

1.

FADE IN

SOMETIME IN THE FUTURE:

INT. ENGINE ROOM

Empty, cavernous.

INT. ENGINE CUBICLE

Circular, jammed with instruments.
All of them idle.
Console chairs for two.
Empty.

INT. OILY CORRIDOR - "C" LEVEL

Long, dark.
Empty.
Turbos throbbing.
No other movement.

INT. CORRIDOR - "A" LEVEL

Long, empty.

INT. INFIRMARY - "A" LEVEL

Distressed ivory walls.
All instrumentation at rest.

INT. CORRIDOR TO BRIDGE - "A" LEVEL

Black, empty.

INT. BRIDGE

Vacant.
Two space helmets resting on chairs.
Electrical hum.
Lights on the helmets begin to signal one another.
Moments of silence.
A yellow light goes on.
Data mind bank in b.g.
Electronic hum.
A green light goes on in front of one helmet.
Electronic pulsing sounds.
A red light goes on in front of other helmet.
An electronic conversation ensues.
Reaches a crescendo.
Then silence.
The lights go off, save the yellow.

INT. CORRIDOR TO HYPERSLEEP VAULT

Lights come on.
Seven gowns hang from the curved wall.
Vault door opens.

INT. HYPERSLEEP VAULT

Explosion of escaping gas.
The lid on a freezer pops open.
Slowly, groggily, KANE sits up.
Pale.
Kane rubs the sleep from his eyes.
Stands.
Looks around.
Stretches.
Looks at the other freezer compartments.
Scratches.
Moves off.

INT. GALLEY

Kane plugs in a Silex.
Lights a cigarette.
Coughs.
Grinds some coffee beans.
Runs some water through.

                    KANE
          Rise and shine, Lambert.

INT. HYPERSLEEP VAULT

Another lid pops open.
A young woman sits up.

                  LAMBERT
            What time is it?

                    KANE
               (voice over)
            What do you care?

INT. GALLEY

Pot now half-full.
Kane watches it drip.
Inhales the fragrance.

                    KANE
          Now Dallas and Ash.
               (calls out)
          Good morning Captain.

                  DALLAS
               (voice over)
            Where's the coffee.

                    KANE
               Brewing.

LAMBERT walks into the kitchen.
Pours herself a cup.

INT. HYPERSLEEP VAULT

Two more lids pop open.
A pair of men sit up.
Look at each other.

INT. GALLEY

Kane enjoys a freshly-brewed cup.

                    KANE
          Ripley...

Another moment.
And then the sound of another lid opening.

                    KANE
          And if we have Parker, can
          Brett be far behind.

Lid opening sound.

                    KANE
          Right.

INT. HYPERSLEEP VAULT

DALLAS looks at his groggy circus.

                    DALLAS
          One of you jokers get the
          cat.

RIPLEY picks up a limp cat out of one of the
compartments.

INT. MESS

The crew of the United States commercial starship
Nostromo seated around a table. [4]

    Television sit-coms double-space everything. Although they aren't the purview of this book, here's a sample, so you'll recognize it if you decide to try writing for television:

                    JERRY

          There's a naked woman across

          the street.

ELAINE

Oh. (LAUGHS) This is gonna

be the easiest money I've

ever made in my life...so

my friend Joyce started

teaching aerobics. I might

take a class later.

BUT JERRY AND GEORGE ARE DISTRACTED BY THE WOMAN
ACROSS THE STREET.

JERRY

(TO ELAINE) Well, the

waitress should've taken it

back.

ELAINE

So then I got a call this

morning. You know, I was

chosen to go on the space

shuttle. We're going to

Mars.

JERRY

Uh huh...

GEORGE

Have a good time.

<u>KRAMER ENTERS</u> CARRYING A ROLL OF CASH. HE SLAPS IT
ON THE COUNTER.

                    KRAMER

          I'm out.

                    ELAINE

          What?

                    KRAMER

          Yeah, I'm out. I'm out of

          the contest.

                    GEORGE

          You're out?

                    KRAMER

          I'm out.

                    ELAINE

          Wow, that was fast.

                    KRAMER

          Well, it was that woman

          across the street. (TO

          JERRY) You know, you better

          be careful, buddy, she's

          gonna get you next.

<u>HE EXITS.</u>

```
                    ELAINE

        And then there were three.

                              CUT TO: ⁵
```

Don't justify right hand margins.

```
It  can make  too many  of  your  lines look  like
this,  which   hurts   the  reader's rhythm and
looks             very               stupid.
```

Page breaks

If description carries over onto the next page, it doesn't need any special notation. However, some scriptwriting software can automatically end your last sentence before the page turn, rather than ending a page on an incomplete sentence.

If dialogue needs to carry over on to the next page, write (MORE) at the bottom, then repeat the character name at the top of the next page, followed by (cont'd).

```
              SAM
    We didn't believe your
    story, Mrs. O'Shaughnessy,
    we believed your 200
    dollars.
        (MORE)
```

```
              SAM (cont'd)
    I mean you paid us more than
    if you had been telling us
    the truth, and enough more
    to make it alright. ⁶
```

Don't use (CONTINUED) at the top and bottom of each page.

You're wasting four lines. Anyone reading your screenplay who doesn't know he's supposed to turn the page is a numskull. That's correct only for production scripts, when a numbered scene carries over a page.

•   •   •

 Maybe now is a good time to discuss the difference between a production script and a spec or assignment screenplay.

As defined by William Goldman in his outstanding book on the movie business, *Adventures in the Screen Trade* (Warner Books, 1983), there are two kinds of screenplays: reading and shooting. He says that when you're writing a screenplay, make it *readable*. This is especially good advice for a writer working on spec and hoping to sell the thing. Later, if the film goes into pre-production, the screenplay will be boarded and budgeted. The production draft will have CONTINUEDS and scene numbers and other esoteric things that writers tend to like, as it gives them a feeling of being in the business, instead of on the outside with their nose pressed against the window. But you are trying to *sell* a screenplay, so make it a smooth read.

Not too long ago all screenplays read like shooting scripts, with lots of close-ups and camera angles and scene numbers. Compare the first page of this 1971 screenplay—

```
EXT. LE VALLON

Opening shot - High angle on Lincoln along small
bay with boats.

EXT. BAR - Waist to Full Figure Pan Right to Left.

Detective comes out eating pizza, looking around.
He crosses street and stops against wall of Impasse
Michel.

He looks O.S. Left
```

HIS POV - L.S. of Lincoln behind fishing nets.

Waist shot of Detective looking and eating.

M.S. of Lincoln

C.S. of Detective looking O.S. Left.

Pan Right to Left with Charnier coming out from Fanfon with three friends and they walk to the Lincoln.

Pan Left to Right with Lincoln passing in front of the Detective.

EXT. CAFE LA SAMARITAINE

High angle from balcony. Zoom on Detective seated at the cafe, reading a newspaper.

Cut on Lincoln along sidewalk of the cafe, then zoom back to discover Detective seated.

EXT. MARSEILLE STREETS

Low Angle from stairs Rue des Repenties and Pan Left to Right to Rue Sainte Francoise following the Detective.

Pan Left to Right with Detective from Rue des Repenties to Rue Baussenque.

Low Angle between Rue des Moulins and Rue des Accoules with detective passing by.

EXT. RUE DU PANIER - the Detective comes out from the bakery Camera Right and starts to climb up Rue des Moulins with his bread. [7]

—with this 1987 screenplay's first page:

EXT. DETROIT - DARK STREET

This is the bad part of town - Old Detroit. Once a manufacturer's paradise, now an industrial ruin.

Two Turbocruisers rumble by slowly. These vehicles, short stubby cars built over twin turbines, are all business. Spotlight plays across alleys and doorways.

INT. TURBOCRUISER 143

Two cops, SPIVY and ALCOTT, monitor an impressive array of electronics spread across the dashboard. Readouts pump cop information. Nervous chatter comes over the radio. These guys are dressed for heavy urban crime: They wear padded body suits, high-impact plastic chest armor etched in black and white, and sleek black helmets with built in visors.

> SPIVY
> (helmet radio)
> What was that?

EXT. GUTTED STOREFRONT

The spotlight plays across crumbling facades and piles of garbage burning brighter than daylight. A SHADOW FIGURE darts from alleyway to door. The spotlight catches him for a moment but then he is gone.

INT. TURBOCRUISER 217

Two more cops, FREDERICKSON and CONNORS, watch the lead car slow up ahead.

> FREDERICKSON
> (driving)
> Whad'ya got, Little Sister?

> ALCOTT (O.S.)
> My God...it's a woman.

Connors looks at Frederickson.

```
INT. TURBOCRUISER 143
```

```
Alcott and Spivy are sharing a private joke.
```

```
                ALCOTT
              (continuing)
          ...Jesus, pinch me Spivy, am
          I crazy or is she wearing a
          bikini?
```

```
                SPIVY
          She's holding a sign...Uh,
          it's says..."Let's play
          circus." 8
```

Clearly the style today avoids camera talk to concentrate on story and character. Perhaps writers have finally realized that directors and cinematographers will do whatever they want anyway.

(cont'd)

The use of a (cont'd) when a character is still talking but has been interrupted by action or description is up to you. Until recently it was de rigueur, as in:

```
Harry spits a grape seed out the window, which
doesn't happen to be down.
```

```
                HARRY
          I'll roll down the window.
```

```
After a lengthy silence.
```

```
                HARRY (cont'd)
          Why don't you tell me the
          story of your life? 9
```

But lately I've noticed that, in the interest of as few words and as clean a page as possible, some good writers are not using it.

Don't number your scenes.

Again, that's for a production script that is to be boarded and budgeted.

Number your pages on the top right hand corner.

Put a period after the page number, so when scene numbers are added, they can be distinguished from page numbers.

Go ahead, put in the opening credits.

A good many screenplays make no mention of the opening titles. There isn't anything wrong with this, so it isn't a *don't*. But you are wasting a good few minutes of screen time, and you leave yourself open to letting the director or producer put them in wherever and however they want. They will anyway, but if you've got a good idea, say so.

All you have to say is—

TITLES OVER

—followed by a scene, or a description of a montage, or whatever you like. Where you want the last credit (contractually the director's), write—

LAST CREDIT FADES OUT

—or—

MAIN TITLES FINISH

—or something appropriate.

Don't spell them out or drag them out. You might even have some credits over scene one, none over scene two, some more over scene three, none over scene four, and etc. But **don't** go on too long, and **don't** say what they are.

Here's a nice scene with little dialogue and lots of visuals that works well under its credits:

FADE IN:

EXT. DESERT OF THE AMERICAN SOUTHWEST - DAY

A mountain peak dominates the landscape.

TITLES BEGIN.

Riders on horseback cross the desert. From this
distance they appear to be a company of Army
Cavalry Soldiers.

CLOSER ANGLES ON THE RIDERS

reveal only details of saddles, hooves and
uniforms. The riders are silhouetted against the
rising sun as they ride into an ancient CLIFF
PUEBLO.

The OFFICER IN COMMAND raises his hand halting his
troops.

                    OFFICER
                Dis-mount!

RIDERS climb down from their mounts...and only now
do we realize that this is a TROOP OF BOY SCOUTS,
all of them about thirteen years of age. The
"Commanding Officer" is only their SCOUTMASTER, Mr.
Havelock.

One of the Scouts, a pudgy kid named HERMAN, steps
away from his horse, bends over and pukes. The
other Scouts rag on him.

                FIRST SCOUT
            Herman's horsesick!

A BLOND SCOUT, however, befriends Herman. He has a
thatch of straw-colored hair and the no-nonsense
expression common to kids whose curiosity and
appetite for knowledge exceed what they teach in
school. Additionally, he has adorned his uniform
with an authentic HOPI INDIAN WOVEN BELT.

                    SCOUTMASTER
          Chaps, don't anybody wander
          off. Some of the passageways
          in here can run for miles.

Two Boy Scouts climb up the rocky base of the
cliff.

INT. THE PASSAGEWAY - DAY

The two boys head down the passageway. It's dark,
and the temperature drops several degrees. Spiders
have built huge webs that get caught in the boys'
hair.

HERMAN appears very uncertain as to the wisdom of
this enterprise, but he's drawn on by his
companion's adventurous curiosity.

                    HERMAN
          I don't think this is such a
          good idea.

LAUGHTER is HEARD; the Blond Scout pulls Herman
forward toward its source.

The VOICES GROW LOUDER now as the boys get closer
to their source. The light of kerosene lanterns
dances on the tunnel walls ahead. The boys approach
cautiously, careful to stay hidden.

                    HERMAN
          What is it?

This is what they see:

FOUR MEN digging with shovels and pick-axes. They
have broken into one of the pueblo's SECRET
CHAMBERS...called "Kivas."

The men are ROUGH RIDER (his name describes his
dress), ROSCOE (a Bowery Boy bully of 14) and
HALFBREED (with straight black hair that cascades
over his shoulders).

And the fourth man wears a LEATHER WAIST JACKET and BROWN FELT FEDORA HAT. He has his back turned to us, but we would be willing to bet anything that this is INDIANA JONES.

However, when the man turns, and his face is illuminated by the lantern's glow, we are shocked to discover that it is someone else.

We'll call him FEDORA.

TITLES END.

The TWO BOYS are mesmerized by what they see.

Now we realize that the Blond Scout is actually young INDIANA JONES. [10]

Here's a briefer scene with good cinematic power.

BEGIN MAIN TITLE SEQUENCE:

An impressionistic montage:

A SILHOUETTED MAN in front of mirror dons his Marine dress blues. Spit polish shoes laced. Medals clipped to jacket. All in CLOSE-UP. We never see him fully.

The Man puts HIS HAT squarely on his head. EYES glint.

On the man's dresser: MARINE MEMORABILIA. Three Purple Hearts, photos of a WOMAN (his wife), PHOTOS OF MARINES in combat locales. TIGHTER into the photos, we HEAR PANICKED VOICES, EXPLOSIONS, NOISES OF BRUTAL COMBAT.

IMAGES: Through smoke, a desperate MARINE PRIVATE who knows he will never be rescued...TWO MARINES walk up to a farmhouse door; through the screen we see a MOTHER AND DAUGHTER who know what the news will be...

```
IMAGES: A MARINE COLOR GUARD carries a COFFIN...Now
we are the coffin as a FLAG drapes down on us. The
flag is placed into a YOUNG WOMAN'S HAND.

Now we're in ARLINGTON CEMETERY. Images of the
cemetery are reflected in wet puddles, as the SPIT-
SHINED SHOES walk past images of the TOMB OF THE
UNKNOWN SOLDIER a ROW OF GRAVES comes into focus.

CLOSE-UP on the MARINE'S HAT, and his EYES.
Suddenly AN EXPLOSION and we see —

A MARINE in a jungle, radioing for help: "You
gotta get us outta here sir, Jesus, they're all
over us...!" And an EXPLOSION ends the
communication...

CLOSE-UP on the MARINE'S EYES and FADE IN:

EXT. ARLINGTON NATIONAL CEMETERY - MORNING ¹¹
```

And the film begins.

Another useful gimmick is to open with a riveting scene right away, THEN go to credits, otherwise known as the "James Bond" opening. Here it's used cleverly:

```
FADE IN

INT. MOUNTAIN CABIN - DAY

A size 16-EEE boot kicks through the door, ripping
the old board from the wall. GROGAN'S grisly body
stands framed in the doorway, a dirty foul-smelling
beast. The shotgun in his grip is cocked. A strong-
hearted beauty, ANGELINA, 34, in buckskin poncho,
eyes him guardedly from behind a table and
surreptitiously slides a boot dagger out of its
sheath. In the rafters a spider faints.

FLIES BUZZ the smoked hides hanging from the beams,
something simmers in the pot over the fire. In the
distance are HEARD THE TUMBLING WATERS of the South
Fork of the Flathead River. All else is mountain
stillness. It is 1850.
```

Grogan clears trail dust from his throat.

>   GROGAN
>   What's it gonna be,
>   Angelina?

The woman does not blink. Grogan, with shotgun
aimed at her breast, swaggers over to the pot,
one-handedly fills the ladle, gulps its contents.

>   GROGAN
>   (spitting it out)
>   What the hell _is_ that?

>   ANGELINA
>   Leftovers.

>   GROGAN
>   (throwing down the
>   ladle)
>   You can die two ways, Angel.
>   Quick like snake tongue or
>   slower than molasses in
>   January.

>   ANGELINA
>   It's April.

>   GROGAN
>   I'd kill ya if it was the
>   goddamn Fourth of July.
>   Where is it?

Grogan's beady eyes dart about the room and lock
onto the saddle-bags on the bunk. With one graceful
movement, Angelina grabs the dagger's tip and flips
it underhand; in a silver flash the dagger cuts
through the air and kills Grogan deader than George
Washington.

Angelina snatches up the shotgun.

ANGELINA (V.O.)
For a moment I stared at
Grogan, the man who killed
my father, raped and
murdered my sister, burned
my ranch, shot my dog, and
stole my bible.

She hoists the saddlebags over her shoulder and
heads out.

CUT TO:

EXT. CABIN

S.O. "ANGELINA'S THEME"

Angelina runs to the top of a small rise, and as
the breeze blows her hair, she pauses to scout the
area. Seeing nothing, she scrambles down toward a
canoe at river's edge.

ANGELINA (V.O.)
The hunt was far from over.
Now Grogan's brothers would
come for me.

CUT TO:

EXT. CAVE

Six of the meanest outlaws in the history of the
west, the BROTHERS, in matching ankle-length coats,
on stallions, come at a THUNDERING gallop out of a
cave, pull up short, squinting into the sun,
seeing, recognizing (the hat particularly)

ANGLE

a man on horseback on the crest of a ridge,
silhouetted against the afternoon sun.

>   ANGELINA (V.O.)
>   But Jack would stop them. He
>   promised me that. It was the
>   only thing the man ever
>   promised.

CLOSE ON

his eyes. The man is JACK COLTON, about 40. On the
rim of legend, he *is* a Willie Nelson/Waylon
Jennings song. And were cowboys immortalized on
bubble gum cards, one Jack Colton would be worth
four Doc Holidays, six Wyatt Earps, eight Buffalo
Bills, and 740 Roy Rogers!

ANGLE

The Brothers riding like hell back into the cave.

>   CUT TO:

RIVER

After stowing her gear; Angelina pushes off.

>   ANGELINA (V.O.)
>   Time to head South. Time to
>   forget.

The canoe is grabbed by the sudden current.
Thundering southward, the river turns into a raging
white roller coaster. A wind comes up, GROWING
LOUDER with each twist of the river, growing until
it sounds like winter's last stand.

>   ANGELINA (V.O.)
>   I started laughing. The
>   world was stark mad, and I
>   was laughing. But not alone.
>   The wind laughed, too. In
>   fact, howled. With each bend
>   in the—

>   CUT TO:

IN CLOSE ON PAGE IN TYPEWRITER. APT. - DAY

                    ANGELINA (V.O.)
          riber —

Angelina pronounces the word exactly as it is
mistyped. A self-correcting IBM selectric
backtracks, lifting the last three letters off the
page, replacing them with "ver."

A cigarette is snuffed in an ashtray sporting a
die-cast "Statue of Liberty." This Statue of
Liberty belongs to JOAN CHARLES, age 34.

ROLL CREDITS.

Though Joan Charles is the woman playing Angelina,
she is her antithesis. Introverted, cloaked in drab
garments, an unnatural hair style - she is barely
recognizable. Joan Charles has the look of a woman
who has forgotten herself, forgotten she has a life
of her own.

Surrounded by globes, books, maps tacked to
bulletin boards and endless stacks of *National
Geographics*, she pauses for a hit of coffee. The
cup is empty.

ANGLE

Heading for the kitchen she passes her exercycle
and the framed cover art of her previous novels:
"The Savage Secret," "Wicked Loving Kisses," "The
Ravengers," and "The Return of Angelina," She also
passes two family photographs.

CLOSE ON

Joan with her parents, Joan with her sister,
Elaine.

ANGLE

In the kitchen she checks the empty coffee tin, checks the time, and checks the schedule taped to the refrigerator door. Every hour is filled with either reading, writing, eating, or exercise.

                              CUT TO:

LOBBY - NEW YORK APARTMENT BUILDING

Trudging down the bottom flight, bundled up for winter's assault, Joan is heading for the exit when she accidentally catches her eye in the lobby mirror. Her own image has never pleased her, and having never looked like the person she thinks she is, she quickly looks away.

ANGLE

When Joan opens the front door a howl of wind and snow whirls in.

                              CUT TO:

EXT. BUILDING

Hunched over, Joan turns down the block into the storm as a taxi pulls up. Through its window we SEE A MAN in sunglasses, Panama, and white linen suit lean forward to pay the fare.

ANGLE

Bent into the wind, the small figure that is Joan Charles, dark against winter's white, disappears up the frozen street as a FLURRY OF SNOW nearly obscures her from view.

END CREDITS

                              CUT TO: [12]

As for the end titles crawl, you needn't remark on that at all, unless you have a specific image or images you want to hold on while they roll. *Young Sherlock Holmes* showed a long, live action scene under the final crawl, then announced the sequel. (It flopped, and a sequel was never made.) *Planes, Trains, and Automobiles* actually had a scene *after* the final credits. A controversial idea. In the theatre, the vast majority of the audience was heading for their cars when the scene played. Outtakes have become popular for comedies, but self-aggrandizement like that seems to me to negate the suspension-of-disbelief good filmmakers work hard to achieve.

Scene Sluglines
Don't put the names of characters into your scene slugline.

```
INT. HOUSE - CATHARINE AND AGNES - DAY
```

This was standard for a long time. But so was a screenplay format that spelled out every single shot and angle. Screenplays like that stem from the halcyon days of the studio system, when writers were paid weekly (oh, glorious time) to write movies, and were descended from the silent movie scenario (when the writer had to do *something* for his money). Today a slugline needs *only* three things—

1. `INT.` or `EXT.` An abbreviation for interior and exterior, this is really a convention for the production manager, and lately I've noticed screenwriters cutting down on these very successfully. If you are in, for example—

```
INT. A HOUSE - DAY
```

—then subsequent scenes in the house need only be identified as

```
BATHROOM
```

—or—

```
MASTER BEDROOM
```

—or—

```
KITCHEN.
```

Only if you go away and come back do you need to re-establish a full slugline.

2. YOUR SETTING, followed by a dash. This can be anything from A HOUSE to THE TAJ MAHAL, but keep it brief. If it requires a lot of explanation, save that for the description.

3. DAY or NIGHT is traditional. This gives the reader a time frame, the lighting designer a hint about lights, and the production manager help with scheduling—usually all night scenes are scheduled together, so the crew's sleeping habits get screwed up only once in a shoot. It can be varied for specificity. You could use

- MORNING

—or—

- THE NEXT MORNING

—or—

- DUSK

—or—

- MIDNIGHT

—or—

- DAY, WINTER, 1912

—or—

- CONTINUOUS

if the scene is the same as the last one. Or even

- DECEMBER 21, 1947

if you're writing an historically accurate screenplay.

DAY FOR NIGHT

is one of those neat film terms (and the title of a wonderful Truffaut film). It means that the scene takes place at night, but it's shot during the day. But you needn't decide such things in your screenplay, and it will only confuse a reader. If it's nighttime, just put NIGHT and let the producer worry about when it will be shot.

These three items should be *in that order*, e.g.:

EXT. THE URUBAMBA RIVER - DUSK

INT. INDY'S OFFICE, SMALL EASTERN COLLEGE - DAY

INT. "THE RAVEN" SALOON - PATAN, NEPAL - NIGHT

EXT. HOK'S STREET - IN FRONT OF PALACE - DAY

EXT. ALLEY BEHIND HOK'S MUSEUM - DAY

INT. DINING ROOM - SALLAH'S HOUSE (OLD CAIRO)

INT. THE WELL OF THE SOULS [13]

The eye sees INT. or EXT. right away, and that triggers an automatic response in the mind of the experienced screenplay reader. It tells us that what follows is a new scene, or at least a new setting.

A corollary to this rule is to *not* use it if you *do not* want to make a change in the scene. In other words, we're reading quickly (never forget that) and INT. or EXT. means a jump to another, if related, place. But not a match cut (a cut between two shots which share something in common) or a reverse angle. If we haven't gone anywhere, just turned the camera around, don't write INT. or EXT.

As for characters traveling from one place to another, you might write—

INT. BAR - NIGHT

He sees her leave. He gets up and follows her.

EXT. BAR - NIGHT

He is on her heels as she leaves the front door of the bar.

—and that would be technically correct. But you've created the impression of a new scene when actually you want the continuity of the man following the girl outside. Eventually, the director might shoot the whole thing through the window for all you know, or track the camera right through the door with them. At any rate, it may or may not be a cut and certainly it isn't a new scene. So write:

```
INT. BAR - NIGHT

He sees her leave. He follows her.

EXT. BAR - CONTINUOUS

He follows her up the street.
```

and the CONTINUOUS clues us in. Better yet might be:

```
INT. BAR - NIGHT

He sees her leave. He gets up and follows her

OUTSIDE

where he follows her up the street.
```

Here's an example of the overuse of INT. or EXT.

```
INT. NICK'S CAR

Nick sees a police car coming toward him.

EXT. NICK'S CAR

Nick turns sharply at a high speed. He skids past a
mausoleum, nearly smashing into it.

EXT. POLICE CAR

It misses the turn and crashes into the mausoleum
knocking through the thick wall.

INT. NICK'S CAR

He glances in the rear view mirror.
```

ANGLE - REAR VIEW MIRROR

The two police cars, one behind the other, in hot pursuit. Galloway in the lead car.

EXT. NICK'S CAR

The roadway ahead of Nick dead ends at the wall surrounding the cemetery.

Nick turns off the roadway into a walkway between the two rows of graves. He drives on, parallel to the wall.

EXT. POLICE CARS

They turn into the walkway and drive after Nick.

CLOSE ANGLE—THE TIRES OF NICK'S CAR

pursuing Nick through the narrow walkway. The wheels of the second car scrape the stone borders of several graves. A tire BLOWS and the car goes out of control. It comes to a stop against a gravestone.

Here's a much better way of describing the same scene:

THE CHASE

Nick sees a police car coming toward him.

He turns sharply at a high speed. He skids past a mausoleum, nearly smashing into it.

The police car misses the turn and crashes into the mausoleum knocking through the thick wall.

Nick glances in the rear view mirror: the two police cars, one behind the other, in hot pursuit. Galloway in the lead car.

The roadway ahead of Nick dead ends at the wall surrounding the cemetery.

```
Nick turns off the roadway into a walkway between
the two rows of graves. He drives on, parallel to
the wall.

The police cars turn into the walkway and drive
after Nick, passing through the narrow walkway. The
wheels of the second car scrape the stone borders
of several graves. A tire BLOWS and the car goes
out of control. It comes to a stop against a
gravestone.
```

All I've really done is take out a lot of unnecessary sluglines. This makes for much easier reading, and saves you a number of lines.

Tell the reader where the story takes place.

You can use the slugline, as in:

```
EXT. 59TH AND MADISON, NEW YORK CITY - DAY
```

or not, as in

```
EXT. INTERSECTION - DAY

Rush hour in New York City's financial district.
```

or just

```
EXT. BIG CITY - DAY
```

if you want to be generic. Usually, we like to know where we are, either with specific, real place names, or with descriptions. Even if your story has everything to do with characters and nothing to do with locale, all films benefit from setting. A simple love story plays differently in a small Vermont town in the depths of winter than it does in Palm Desert. If you really do not want to say precisely where, at least do not forget to describe the kind of town or place you want.

Keep in mind what you've chosen while you write your scenes. Does vapor come from a speaker's mouth? Are lips parched? Do we trip on long woolen scarves or admire nearby girls in scant bikinis? Is the view breathtaking? Are the streets dangerous? A film is a visual experience. If you've only written dialogue, you've only written half a movie.

Transitions

The most common transition of all is—

                                        CUT TO:

—as in:

Under the car, BUCKAROO BANZAI pulls an alien life
form off of the drive shaft.

                                        CUT TO:

DR. LIZARDO's room at the Trenton Home for the
Criminally Insane. [14]

However, most authors use it very sparingly, as it lengthens a script unnecessarily. Provided the next scene starts with a slugline, the reader will know a new scene is beginning, and CUT TO isn't needed. For example:

She sits, quietly, looking at him. Cautiously, she
brings his hand to her cheek. A slight smile
crosses her face.

INT. MAIN ROOM, THX'S QUARTERS

THX is laughing hysterically. As soon as he starts
to gain control of himself, he breaks out laughing
again. [15]

That also saves you a line. One of my pet peeves is

                                        SMASH CUT TO:

—or—

                                        SLAM CUT TO:

These are increasingly popular, especially in television. No such thing exists. A cut is a cut; you cannot cut any faster than from one frame to one frame. That is a CUT. You can cut slower, overlapping any number of frames, which would be a DISSOLVE. You can FADE OUT and then FADE IN. But you cannot cut any faster. The effect the author is going for here is probably one of sudden juxtaposition, or shock. The best way to write that is to have the first scene well written and ending cleanly, followed by the next, written just as cleanly. If you write, for example—

She opens the door slowly, fearfully.

IN THE CLOSET

A MAN hangs there, his swollen tongue the first thing we see.

—then clearly we are going for a screamer of a cut and the editor will make it work. Or not. But you can't help by writing an indication for something that does not really exist. If you're really anxious to make a sudden transition, give the editor a hint by writing:

ABRUPT CUT TO:

That says you want the scene virtually interrupted, and the next shot should startle us.

- FADE OUT and FADE IN

There is nothing wrong with these, as long as they are not overused. More than a handful of fades in a screenplay is going to look like one very slow movie. Bear in mind that coming out of a fade will cause the audience to assume that significant time has elapsed and we are somewhere else.

- DISSOLVE

Very little real dissolving is done in movies these days. It is an old fashioned way of indicating a dream sequence, a montage, or the passage of time. But if you want a flashback or a slow transition, it's valid.

• The Content Transition

Good transitions convey information. A good screenplay moves from scene to scene much more smoothly with their use:

```
                    WILLIAM
          I wish I were in Hawaii.


                              CUT TO:


EXT. HAWAII - DAY

Palm trees and trade winds. William sits in a
hammock, smiling.
```

—or—

```
A GIRL carefully packs a suitcase in her room.
Finished, she looks around, giving one last wistful
glance at the things from her childhood she has
left behind. Finally she closes her suitcase and
snaps the locks. We CLOSE IN on the suitcase.


                              CUT TO:


CLOSE ON the suitcase being pulled from the luggage
compartment of a bus. We are in

EXT. BUS STATION - DAY

A DRIVER takes the suitcase down. The girl hefts
it, and looks around at the crowded city.
```

—or—

```
A young BOY is pitching a baseball at the side of a
barn.


                              CUT TO:


THE BOY GROWN UP, pitching in the big leagues.
```

—or—

```
CHICAGO. A COW is being butchered in a
slaughterhouse.
```

```
                                    CUT TO:
```

```
NEW YORK. A MAN is carving into his steak.
```

These are the best transitions because they are content based.

    Transitions based on content can also tell us events without having to spell them out. We make assumptions on intervening activity. In the examples above, William went to Hawaii, the girl traveled to New York, the kid grew up to play major league ball, and the cow. . .well, not all stories have a happy ending.

• The Time Transition.

Some screenplays cover a lot of ground, and you'll need transitions to let us know that time has passed, and sometimes how much. The classic time-passing cut is two takes on a clock, or a calendar. You can do better. Deal with the real events of your story and not the props.

    Here "Reese" is making half a dozen bombs, and the material is laid out on the table:

```
...he turns her wrist to read her watch.
```

```
                REESE
        We'll head out at 0200.
        That gives you four hours to
        sleep if you want. I'll
        finish.
```

```
                                    CUT TO:
```

```
INT. MOTEL ROOM - NIGHT
```

```
ANGLE ON TABLE - The bombs are neatly stacked,
finished. A nylon satchel lies nearby. The mess is
cleaned up.
```

```
WIDE SHOT reveals Reese sitting in silent vigil at
the  window. The room is dark, lit only by a
streetlight  outside.  Sarah is asleep on the bed. ¹⁶
```

We know at once he's finished his work, and it's getting time to put their plan in motion. Here's an even simpler time transition:

```
INT. ALEX'S STUDIO - NIGHT

The two of them are lying naked in front of the
fire.

ALEX'S STUDIO - NEXT MORNING

A bitterly cold dawn. ¹⁷
```

And here is the simplest of all:

```
LATER
```

Use it when you don't have a transition. It is clear that you are leaving it to the editor, and you have not resorted to a cliché.

• The Comic Transition.

```
          BURKE
     Just tell them what
     happened. The important
     thing is to stay cool and
     unemotional.

INT. CONFERENCE ROOM

She's not cool. Not unemotional.

          RIPLEY
     Do you people have earwax,
     or what? We have been here
     three hours. How many
     different ways do you want
     me to tell the same story? ¹⁸
```

Nothing wrong with a good laugh. This one goes back decades:

```
              PRESIDENT
        ...My staff and I are
        remaining here at the
        White House while we attempt
        to establish communication
        ...so remain calm. If you
        are compelled to leave these
        cities, please do so in a
        safe and orderly fashion.


                         CUT TO:


CABS SLAMMING TOGETHER - NEW YORK CITY STREETS ¹⁹
```

• The Aural Transition
This kind of cut should almost never be put into your script. Leave it for the editor. Aural transitions make sense on the screen, and are used by editors to speed the film along, but seen on paper they are confusing. If the scene reads—

```
Jim sits alone in his apartment thinking. The phone
rings.


                         CUT TO:


INT. BILL'S APARTMENT - NIGHT

Bill picks up his telephone.
```

—then we tend to think that the phone is ringing in Jim's room. Editors can time this so we only subconsciously feel the overlap, without being confused, but it is difficult to do on paper. Stick to finding good transitions based on content whenever possible. Use the aural transition very carefully, and only when you are confident the reader will immediately understand that the sound is a preview of the upcoming scene.

You **don't need a content-based transition at every scene change.** But go through your script. If you don't find a single one, look for a few opportunities. If there's too many, or they're labored and artificial, go for something simpler.

Don't use CUT TO unless it's a new scene. For example, this is absurd:

```
                    SAM
          So you're Bill's sister.

                                        CUT TO:


                    MARY
          That's me.

                                        CUT TO:


                    SAM
          I've heard about you.

                                        CUT TO:


                    MARY
          What have you heard?
```

You've seen a lot of movies where each of the characters gets plenty of close-ups, but that's cinematography, not screenwriting.

The rule then, is to use CUT TO only when jumping to a new scene. And if you use a slugline, all in caps, you don't necessarily even need that.

Even when the two characters in conversation are on the telephone, you don't need:

```
INT. PAULA'S APARTMENT - NIGHT

Paula, looking official as ever, sits behind a
small desk. She talks into the telephone.

                    PAULA
          Mary, are you asleep?

                                        CUT TO:

INT. MARY'S APARTMENT - NIGHT

Mary is sleeping. Groggily she holds the receiver.
```

                    MARY
              (through sleep)
        No.

                              CUT TO:

INT. PAULA'S APARTMENT - NIGHT

                    PAULA
        Good.
              (a beat)
        I want to help you, Mary.

                              CUT TO:

INT. MARY'S APARTMENT - NIGHT

Mary listens, nods.

                    MARY
        Okay, yes. I can do that. I
        have everything.

She hangs up the phone.

Instead, you can start with the phone ringing—

INT. COMPUTER ROOM - BURPLESON AFB - NIGHT

A phone buzzes.

                    PETTY OFFICER
        General Ripper, sir.

                    MANDRAKE
              (to phone on his desk)
        Group Captain Mandrake
        speaking...

—then bring in the caller, whose "set" we've already seen—

Ripper sits at his desk, cigar smoke wafting up
through the light of his desk lamp.

```
          RIPPER
     (to phone)
This is General Ripper
speaking.
```

—and then just continue their dialogue through the end of the scene:

```
          MANDRAKE
Yes, sir.

          RIPPER
You recognize my voice,
Mandrake?

          MANDRAKE
I do sir, why do you ask?

          RIPPER
Why do you think I asked?

          MANDRAKE
Well I don't know, sir. We
spoke just a few moments ago
on the phone, didn't we?

          RIPPER
You don't think I'd ask if
you recognized my voice
unless it was pretty damned
important do you, Mandrake?

          MANDRAKE
No, I don't, sir. No.

          RIPPER
Alright, let's see if we
stay on the ball. Has the
wing confirmed holding at
their failsafe points?

          MANDRAKE
Yes, sir. The confirmations
have all just come in.
```

>   RIPPER
> Very well, now, listen to me
> carefully. The base is being
> put on condition red. I want
> this flashed to all sections
> immediately.
>
>   MANDRAKE
> Condition red, sir. Yes.
> Jolly good idea, keeps the
> men on their toes.
>
>   RIPPER
> Group Captain, I'm afraid
> this is not a exercise.
>
>   MANDRAKE
> Not an exercise, sir?
>
>   RIPPER
> I shouldn't tell you this,
> Mandrake, but you're a good
> officer and you have a right
> to know. It looks like we're
> in a shooting war. [20]

Who gets which close-up will be left to the editing, and you've written a scene that reads much more fluently.

Angles

If you are not in a new scene, but need to indicate a change of angle, then—

ANGLE on THE GIRL

—is fine. And it has the virtue of identifying what we are supposed to see on the screen at the same time. But overuse is distracting:

>   ROBERT
> You think we ought to go in?

ANGLE ON HARRY

                    HARRY
        Why?

ANGLE ON ROBERT

                    ROBERT
        What do you mean why?

CLOSE ON HARRY

                    HARRY
        Why go in?

In the case of ANGLES or CLOSE UPS, use them sparingly within a scene if you want to draw attention to something:

                BUCKAROO BANZAI
        Is, ahh...is somebody
        ...is somebody crying?
        ...out there in the
        darkness? Somebody crying?

PENNY PRIDDY is visible, sitting alone at a table.

                PENNY PRIDDY
            (sobs)
        Me...I'm sorry...

Long shot of stage. Crowd members are looking back at PENNY PRIDDY, wondering what's going on.

                BUCKAROO BANZAI
        Ummm...could we...could we
        get her a mike? And a
        spotlight? Uh, Tommy, could
        we, uh, could you give her
        your mike?

                PERFECT TOMMY
        Are you serious?

                BUCKAROO BANZAI
        Yeah. Give her your mike.
        (to PENNY PRIDDY) What's
        your name?

                    PENNY PRIDDY
    Who cares?

The crowd is getting fed up with the delay.

                    DRUNK
    Right!

                    BUCKAROO BANZAI
              (sympathetically)
    I care. What's your name?

CLOSE UP of PENNY PRIDDY. She is wearing a short
pink dress and blue gloves. Her makeup is smeared.
She has obviously been crying.

                    PENNY PRIDDY
    Penny. [21]

Use ANGLE or ANGLE ON only when you want to draw
particular attention to something or someone, and *be very* careful
of overusing ANGLES. Unless it's a plot point—

ANGLE top of building. Will she jump?

—leave it for the cinematographer.

The Montage

CUT TO: A series of quick cuts involving Rebecca
and Michael. Music track. Michael sliding out of
the office early, to the envious gaze of his
fellows. Michael shopping at open air markets.
Michael cooking, burning his fingers, sipping wine
at Rebecca's house, then greeting Rebecca apron-
adorned, with drink in hand like Donna Reed.
Michael leading Rebecca after dinner to the couch.
Michael and Rebecca making love.

Michael and Rebecca lying naked (both wearing
glasses) in bed with the paper and coffee, fighting
over a section and then kissing. Michael and
Rebecca riding in the topless Healey down the coast

with the ocean as a backdrop. Having brunch on the
water, walking on the beach. Sneaking under the
pier to sneak a joint with the surfers, giggling
like high schoolers. Watching the sun douse itself
with a flash in the water. Running on the beach,
with Rebecca running easily and Michael travelling
gasping in her wake. Making love again.

That sounds like a great weekend to me, but as screenwriting
goes, it's pretty awful, because there's nothing remotely original
about it, and *because the reader gets lost when you run too many ideas
together*. I was half-way through the above example before I realized
the writer wanted a montage. Here is a much better way of format-
ting the same thing.

MONTAGE:
Michael sliding out of the office early, to the
envious gaze of his fellows.
Michael shopping at open air markets.
Michael cooking, burning his fingers.
Sipping wine at Rebecca's house.
Greeting Rebecca apron-adorned, with drink in hand
like Donna Reed.
Michael leading Rebecca after dinner to the couch.
Michael and Rebecca making love.

—or—

A series of quick cuts involving Rebecca and
Michael.

...Michael sliding out of the office early, to the
envious gaze of his fellows.

...Michael shopping at open air markets.

...Michael cooking, burning his fingers, sipping
wine at Rebecca's house, then greeting Rebecca
apron-adorned, with drink in hand like Donna Reed.

...Michael leading Rebecca after dinner to the
couch.

...Michael and Rebecca making love.

I've also seen more generalized writing, such as

```
A SERIES OF QUICK CUTS
indicate that Michael goes home early, shops for
groceries, cooks dinner for Rebecca, and,
afterwards, leads her to the couch and they make
love.
```

But that's a little skimpy. Probably something in between is best, as this last version leaves too much to the director's imagination. Just bear in mind that you must let the reader know it's a montage of some sort.

Here is the father of all pop song montages:

```
FADE IN:

EXT. BRADDOCK BACKYARD AND POOL AREA - DAY

The midsummer sun beats down on the Braddock
swimming pool and on Ben, who lies on a rubber raft
in the middle of the pool. Ben wears dark glasses,
is deeply tanned, and holds a beer can in one hand.

                          DISSOLVE TO:

CLOSER SHOT of BEN

drifting.

                          DISSOLVE TO:

CLOSER SHOT of BEN

drifting.

                          DISSOLVE TO:

CLOSER SHOT of BEN

Sound of the back door closing. Ben opens his eyes
and moves his head slightly.
```

WHAT HE SEES

Mr. Braddock is passionately stoking a barbecue fire. Mrs. Braddock is going toward him from the house. Carrying some ominously large thing wrapped in tinfoil.

He rolls off the raft and swims to the end of the pool. He climbs out, walks to the back door, takes his shirt from a chair and starts to put it on as he opens the back door and goes through.

INT. TAFT HOTEL ROOM - NIGHT

Ben has just shut the door to the bathroom behind him. He is wearing his shirt, buttoned, and no trousers.

He walks across the room past Mrs. Robinson, who is standing in front of the bureau taking off her bracelet and watch. He moves to a chair and sits.

He picks up a cigarette from an ashtray on a table next to the chair. Mrs. Robinson moves in to Ben, kneels in front of him and starts to unbutton his shirt.

He takes the cigarette out of his mouth.

INT. BRADDOCK DEN AND DINING ROOM - NIGHT

We now see behind Ben the door that leads from the Braddock den, in which Ben is sitting. In the dining room, Mr. and Mrs. Braddock are sitting, having their dinner, looking through the doorway toward Ben. Ben stands, crosses back to the door to the den and shuts it.

On Ben's back as he returns to the chair and sits. A television set, facing the chair, is on. Ben picks up a can of beer and drinks from it. An animated cartoon is playing on the television set. Ben watches it.

REVERSE

Ben's face, watching. PUSH IN to CLOSE UP of his face.

REVERSE

CLOSE UP of television set and cartoon.

REVERSE

BEN watching.

REVERSE

CLOSEUP test pattern.

INT. TAFT HOTEL ROOM - NIGHT

BEN watching. PULL BACK and we are in the Taft Hotel Room. Ben is sitting on the bed, leaning against the headboard, watching the television set which is on a stand facing the bed.

Sound of the hum of the test pattern.

PULL BACK to a WIDE SHOT of the room, lit only by the light from the television set. Mrs. Robinson walks into the shot, half dressed. She passes between Ben and the television set and goes out of frame. Ben continues to stare at the set.

Sound of a zipper being pulled up.

Mrs. Robinson appears again and passes the other way.

Sound of Bracelets being put on.

Mrs. Robinson passes back the other way again.

Sound of clothing being put on and a purse being snapped closed. Mrs. Robinson, now fully dressed and carrying her purse, passes through again and, without looking at Ben, goes to the door of the hotel room, opens it and exits.

INT. BEN'S ROOM - DAY

Sound of a door closing. Follow Ben as he gets up and moves to the windows of what is now his BEDROOM in the Braddock house. He opens the closed blinds over the window. The sun is bright outside. His bathing suit is on the window sill. He takes the suit and puts it on. He moves to the bedroom door, opens it and goes out.

EXT. BRADDOCK BACKYARD AND POOL AREA - DAY

We see Mrs. Braddock in the kitchen. Ben comes through the back door, moves to the pool and dives in. The raft floats in the center of the pool.

UNDERWATER

Ben swims toward us the length of the pool.

AT THE WATER LINE

Ben surfaces and, in one movement, pulls himself up on the raft and

INT. TAFT HOTEL ROOM - NIGHT

- lands on top of Mrs. Robinson on the bed. He stays on top of her for a moment.

> MR. BRADDOCK'S VOICE
> Ben - what are you doing?

Ben turns toward us and looks.

BEN'S POV

Mr. Braddock standing by the side of the pool. The sun is behind him.

```
                    BEN'S VOICE
            Well - I would say that I'm
            just drifting. ²²
```

This is shot by shot specific, takes just three pages—if you envision setting it to most of a song three minutes is about right—demonstrates the fluidity that makes good transitions, and is filled with humor, the essential nature of the loveless assignations, and Benjamin's aimlessness. (Bear in mind that it is also thirty years old, from a time when screenplays tended to be much more shot specific.)

Don't sound like a Batman comic.

```
WE HEAR BREATHING...erratic, heavy, strained. AND
FOOTSTEPS...unsteady footsteps scuffling across
moist and mushy terrain. SCUFFLE, SLOSH, SCUFFLE,
SLOSH. Every now and then the labored breaths
become a GROAN. Slowly the BLACKNESS...
```

Sounds more like instructions for the foley stage than good screenwriting.

Here is a passage-of-time montage (from a purchased screenplay that had to be completely rewritten):

```
CLANG!
```

```
An ancient machine stamps out a calendar: 1982.
```

```
BRING NG NG!
```

```
The bells sound the end of another meal.
```

```
BUZZ Z Z Z
```

```
The buzzers sound taps on another day in the
orphanage.
```

```
BUZZ Z Z Z
```

```
Then Reveille.
```

```
CLANG G G G! 1983!

        CLANG! BANG! SLAM! BUZZ! RING! CLANG!
     SLAM! BUZZ! RING! SLAM! BANG! BUZZ! RING!
   CLANG! BANG! SLAM! BUZZ! RING! CLANG! BANG! SLAM!
   BUZZRINGCLANGBANGSLAMBUZZRINGCLANGBANGSLAMBUZZ!


                       CUT TO:

CLANG!

Another calendar stamped out by our little
overworked orphan. 1985!
```

This is an extreme exaggeration of dumb writing, and I hope you get the idea. Lines like—

```
Sam raises his 9mm Beretta. ZAP, focuses the laser
sight. And BLOWIE! blows the man's head off
```

—are dangerously close to satire.

Trying to put a sound track into words will only read clumsily. We know perfectly well what—

```
SAMMY raises his 9mm Beretta slowly, carefully
sights on his victim, and squeezes the trigger.

ANGLE Sammy's victim: His head blows off.
```

—sounds like. You might even write—

```
The BOOM of the big gun reverberates in the empty
mall.
```

—for effect. Nothing wrong with a little onomatopoeia. But be careful of description that makes your script sound like a comic book. Though comic book pictures may be exactly what the industry is trying to turn out, Hollywood thinks of them as films.

Exclamation marks! CAPITAL LETTERS, <u>underlines</u>, and onomatopoeia like BOOM! can have their uses.
But, like many of the other things we have talked about, the rhythm of the read depends on your writing. Reading is an old habit and CAPITALS tend to EMPHASIZE things. If you overuse ALL CAPS you will not have emphasis when you need it. You might, for example, if you really wanted to bring home a point, say—

```
Then, to the amazement of those watching below, he
LEAPS A TALL BUILDING!
```

—but if you go into the whole Tom Wolfe style of Gonzo journalism, with PINGS and WHIZZZS and CAHOOTS and STUFF!!! Then BE CAREFUL. Too many CAPITAL LETTERS tend to DRIVE the READER a little CRAZY.

One method of description includes putting a lot of things into CAPITAL LETTERS, anything that is a SOUND, from MUSIC, to a SOUND EFFECT, as well as every CHARACTER NAME every time it appears. Although shooting scripts sometimes CAPITALIZE every EFFECT for quick recognition by crafts people, stick to normal prose form as much as possible. When the production people get through prepping a script, if they have missed a special effect or noise because it is in lower and not upper case, it is not your fault.

Capitalize a character's name the first time it appears, but not again. This allows for quick recognition of the introduction of a NEW CHARACTER, but doesn't confuse the issue when several are running around. And you avoid paragraphs like

```
CAROL looks closely at STEVE. STEVE doesn't notice,
for his eye is on DESIRE, now speaking with HAL by
the window. The conversation level is loud enough
to cover the MUSIC, which filters in from the
window over NOISE from the street TRAFFIC.
```

Don't tell the actors which words to punch.

```
                    JENNY
          The minute I don't shine for
          you, you can fire me. But
          I'll be damned if you're
          gonna pass on me because of
          my watch! That's not me.
               (thumps her chest)
          This is me. Guts!
               (pats her temples)
          and brains. You can't do any
          better.
```

That drives a reader crazy. This is not reading aloud. Reading is more in the line of absorbing intent. That little voice in a reader's head tends to bypass histrionics and goes straight to meaning. If the story is good, the reader will be emotionally effected.

Too many stage directions drive actors crazy, and nobody ever follows them. They're just in the way. If your dialogue needs that much thumping up, maybe it really needs polishing instead.

Likewise, don't interpret everything.
Here is an example of very bad screenwriting.

```
He looks up at her.

                    DOROTHY
          What do you find so
          interesting about her?

That calls for an honest answer.

                    AARON
          She has a...remarkable
          personality.

She hears that, but doesn't settle for it.

                    DOROTHY
          That's an easy answer. But
          what else?
```

He loves her. See it again, right here.

> AARON
> (quietly)
> She has a beautiful face.
> But the best part to watch
> is...her mind.

Silence. Too important to pass over.

> DOROTHY
> I had lunch with her this
> week. We talked.

> AARON
> What did she say about me?

He wants to know. She wants to tell him.

> DOROTHY
> To be honest...she doesn't
> much care for you.

There it is. Something compassionate in her voice.
But honest.

This author has interpreted every line of dialogue. Not only does this slow the reader down, fouling up the rhythm of the scene, but it's a dead giveaway that the dialogue is no good. If it were, it would speak for itself. What we have here are acting notes. **Don't put acting notes into your script** unless they are unavoidable. A line like—

> HARRY
> Yeah?

—might require something, unless it's clear in context. In which case, write—

> HARRY
> (cynical)
> Yeah?

—or—

```
          HARRY
       (incredulous)
     Yeah?
```

—or—

```
          HARRY
       (kidding)
     Yeah?
```

—but only to nudge the reader into understanding Harry's intention. Short, parenthetical words or phrases interrupt the flow of your dialogue less than long, descriptive passages, and are sometimes necessary. But try to use them as little as possible. If you have to explain everything you write, re-examine your dialogue.

```
Peter rolls his eyes.
```

Come on. First, this is what actors call "indicating," not acting. People seldom really roll their eyes. An actor expresses an emotion. How he does it is not up to you. Give the actor his activity.

```
Peter is surprised to hear that.
```

Give the actor his character.

```
Peter isn't listening. He could give a shit.
```

Don't tell the actor how to communicate to his audience, tell him what to communicate. Put the character in a situation in which he could, given his character and activity to date, only feel one way, the way you want him to feel. Leave out all indications of how you think the actor should play the scene. Another stinker:

```
          JENNIFER
     You know, my fiancé had his
     eye on this machine for
     years. It's very rare.
```

ALEXIS
Oh, so some lucky guy
convinced you to be his
bride?

Jennifer nods. Alexis smiles flirtatiously.

ALEXIS
So when's the big date?

Jennifer doesn't like this question.

JENNIFER
Don't know.

Alexis lights a cigarette and looks out a window.

ALEXIS
I was engaged once.

JENNIFER
What happened?

Alexis blows a perfect smoke ring.

ALEXIS
He dumped me.

Jennifer looks up from her work.

JENNIFER
Why? I mean, do you mind if
I ask?

Alexis pauses and takes a deep drag of her cig.

ALEXIS
Guess I was just too much
woman for him.

Jennifer smiles at Alexis, thinking she's kidding.
But she's not.

JENNIFER
So what happened?

```
                    ALEXIS
          So I married somebody else.
```

Alexis seems less than excited.

Don't coach an actor on how to say his lines. You'll be wasting precious words. Once a good actor has learned his lines, they are part of his character, not your screenplay. Even the reader is going to create characters in his head and read the lines with whatever inflections come to him. Throwing in acting directions does not do anything but add extraneous words to your screenplay that you do not need, cannot use, and they slow the reader down. Let the dialogue represent the character, and let the actors bring out the character. Here's the same scene, without all the instructions:

```
                 JENNIFER
          You know, my fiancé had his
          eye on this machine for
          years. It's very rare.

                  ALEXIS
          Oh, so some lucky guy
          convinced you to be his
          bride? So when's the big
          date?

                 JENNIFER
          Don't know.

                  ALEXIS
          I was engaged once.

                 JENNIFER
          What happened?

                  ALEXIS
          He dumped me.

                 JENNIFER
          Why? I mean, do you mind if
          I ask?
```

```
              ALEXIS
     Guess I was just too much
     woman for him.


              JENNIFER
     So what happened?


              ALEXIS
     So I married somebody else.
```

Doesn't that read a lot better?

Here's a good example of why we write, and let actors act. Here's the classic orgasm scene from *When Harry Met Sally*, as written in the original script:

```
              HARRY
     You don't think I can tell
     the difference?


              SALLY
     No.


              HARRY
     Please. Don't be ridiculous.
```

Sally just stares at Harry. A seductive look comes
on her face. Slowly she laughs into the beginning
of what builds to be a wild orgasm.

```
              SALLY
     Oh, oh, oh.


              HARRY
     Are you alright?


              SALLY
     Oh, God, oh God, oh yes, oh
     God, great, yes, I'm coming,
     oh - yes, yes, yes! God,
     honey, honey, omiGod, honey,
     oh oh God, oh God, God.
     Thank you.
```

```
Sally finishes, takes another bite of her sandwich.
Smiles innocently.

Hold on Harry, in shock. And the rest of the
customers and the waiters who couldn't help but
overhear Sally's performance.

                    OLDER WOMAN CUSTOMER
                  (to a nearby waiter)
              I'll have what she's having.

                                     FADE OUT. 23
```

Rent the film to see what an actress (of Meg Ryan's caliber) can do with that.

In parentheticals, don't write the obvious:

```
She's disheveled.

He huffs and puffs.
```

A favorite Hollywood cliché is, "Leave room for the actor." It means just that. (And not just about obvious stage directions. Write scenes that aren't "on the nose." Bear in mind that people talk obliquely, seldom saying what they really mean.)

If your character has come in out of the rain, and we know it, stop. Leave the rest up to the director and the actor. And the reader's imagination. If the character has come in out of the rain, but we do not know it, say so.

There is no such thing as (a beat) and using this within dialogue because you want the actor to pause is incorrect.

To be honest, I see this in some very expensive, sometimes very good screenplays, and readers do know what you mean. But the fact remains that a beat is an actor's term, and has nothing to do with timing. It is a definition of the smallest, or shortest, psychological moment. A moment during which the actor says or does something specific with the intention of communicating something to the audience, sometimes without words, but not necessarily. A director might say to an actor, "take a beat here," meaning that, although there is no specific dialogue, there is an intention that needs to be communicated with a look or a small movement.

Well, never mind all that. You can look it up in any acting text. What it ISN'T, is (a pause) and using the terms interchangeably, a very common error, is still an error. You cannot define a beat for an actor. If you are positive you want a pause, then put (pause) in. If you know *why* you want a pause, put in a direction, such as:

```
She stares at the door, tense.
```

—or—

```
Beth waits, hoping he'll introduce himself.
```

—or simply—

```
Bill reacts.
```

But use pauses and reactions sparingly.

The corollary to this is the ellipse. . .it indicates an unfinished sentence or a pause. Use it at the end of a sentence to indicate that the speaker has run out of steam, or is throwing the ball into the other court, as in:

```
          RICHARD
     And you are...?

          AMANDA
     Amanda Jones.

          RICHARD
     I see...
```

But don't overuse it for pauses. Don't write:

```
          RICHARD
     You have a...beautiful
     face...Do you mind...my telling
     you...that...
```

Let the reader find the inner rhythm of the speeches based on the character you have created. Better to write:

```
          RICHARD
     You have a beautiful face.
     Do you mind my telling you
     that?
```

Reading is faster than talking. If you force the reader to read as slowly as your character really speaks, you will bore your poor reader to death. Any reader needing more than one hour to read a two hour screenplay is probably still moving his lips. If anything, readers tend to get the same old ideas, the same cliché characters, the same buddy-cop-romantic-comedy-with-aliens screenplays again and again, and they start speeding up to get to the predictable end. (Of course, you'll avoid this by writing a truly original, non-stereotypical screenplay.)

The exception is the telephone scene, where we only hear one side. Then you may want to indicate the spaces when the actor is listening:

```
The telephone rings. Alvy picks it up, rising up
slightly from the bed, concerned, as he talks.

          ALVY
     Hello...Oh, hi...Uh, no,
     what-what's the matter?
     What-what-what? You sound
     terrible...No, what- Sure I-
     Whatta yuh -what kind of an
     emergency?...No, well,
     there. Stay there, I'll come
     over right now. I'll come
     over right now. Just stay
     there, I'll come right over. 24
```

Don't confuse VOICEOVER (V.O.) with OFF SCREEN (O.S.) or OFF CAMERA (O.C.).

A voice-over is narrative, coming from a character not only <u>not</u> in the shot, but <u>not</u> in the scene:

```
SLOW TRACK over dense cloud cover. Rocky peaks
visible in the distance.

              NARRATOR (V.O.)
         For more than a year,
         ominous rumors have been
         privately circulating among
         high level western leaders,
         that the Soviet Union had
         been at work on what was
         darkly hinted to be the
         ultimate weapon, a doomsday
         device... 25
```

Off screen (O.S.) or off camera (O.C.) indicates
a voice not seen, but in the scene. Such as:

```
INT. CORRIDOR

Stunned, Ripley sees through dissipating smoke the
creature rising to advance again. Flinching against
blast and glare she drills it POINT-BLANK with a
BLINDING BURST that carries the M-41A's muzzle
right up toward the ceiling. Newt covers her ears
against the CONCUSSION.

              HICKS
            (o.s.)
         Hold your fire!

The troopers seem to materialize out of the smoke. 26
```

First person narrative is often utilized, as in:

```
We see a man fall in SLOW MOTION from the top of
the Empire State building.
```

However, you must be very careful not to overuse the audi-
ence-point-of-view idea in screenwriting. It can become strained.
"We see this" and "we see that" and "we follow her" start to smack
of a writer trying too hard. Personally, I would prefer to read:

```
A man falls in SLOW MOTION from the top of the
Empire State building.
```

You can add something more specific by writing:

```
A man falls from the top of the Empire State
building. IN SLOW MOTION, the CAMERA follows him
all the way down.
```

—or—

```
POV from the sidewalk in front of the Empire State
building, looking up. A man falls in SLOW MOTION.
```

If you really need "We" or "Us" to clarify, go ahead, but re-member, however, it must be plural, because you are writing the collective audience POV. **Don't write action or description in first person singular**. In one script I read:

```
I see a ribbon of black asphalt under an azure sky.
I see a motorcycle in the distance.
```

This was terribly confusing, because at first I thought there was a narrator character I was missing. By the time I realized it was a perversion of the usual "We" or the camera, I had already written the screenplay off as inept.

Leave the music track alone.

```
This should be an upbeat scene with a good music
track.
```

(Darn. The studio really wanted to use a bad music track.) Write an upbeat scene, don't describe it.

```
The un-made bed. Introduce an uneasy musical
STINGER. In the BG the SOUND of the shower
continues.
```

I have little idea what an "uneasy musical stinger" is. More important is this: we all know that lately most films are awash in symphonic music telling us what we are supposed to be feeling, usually in lieu of a scene that's not well-written enough to make us feel it. The overuse of melodramatic music is a modern film malaise (encouraged by executives who love to give notes on the mix), but you should avoid it in screenwriting, essentially a silent art.

Unless music is a plot point, you are only cluttering up your screenplay, and the music supervisor and/or composer will probably not read your screenplay if they can avoid it. They may not even be hired until a rough cut is ready.

```
She drives down the street listening to Bonnie
Raitt's "Burning Down the House."
```

Naming songs rarely helps. One, you're wrong. Chances are something else will eventually be chosen. Two, if the reader isn't familiar with your favorite music, it's confusing and meaningless. Three, a reader's orientation is to visual images, and we are not likely to hum along as we read.

Again, if music is a plot point, then it's okay. Screenwriter Richard Price probably chose "Sea of Love" for *Sea of Love* from the beginning.

Don't put in Special Visual Effects.

If a character drinks from a bottle that says "drink me" and suddenly shrinks to a fraction of normal size, it is not necessary to show off your film school degree with things like:

```
F/X: ALICE SHRINKING
```

Just say what happens:

```
Suddenly Alice gets smaller and smaller, until she
is small enough to fit through the little door.
```

Using film jargon like

M.O.S.
ND Car
76 F.P.S.

is not screenwriting. Write what you want us to see:

```
There is no sound.
A late-model car.
In SLOW MOTION
```

Don't divide your screenplay into acts.
Like a film, a screenplay is an uninterrupted drama. A note about teleplays, however:

Network movies-of-the-week have seven acts in two hours, and need to be divided by act breaks (including "Night One" and "Night Two" for a mini-series). The reader is looking for a reason the audience will *not* change the channel on the commercial. Thus there is a large structural difference between a film written for a network—with commercial interruptions—and a film for theatrical release, or a film written for a cable channel that does not have commercials during their programming. If you are writing a network MOW, you must have the requisite suspenseful tags on your go-to-commercial scenes.

Length
Fewer than eighty pages is not long enough. More than one hundred forty is too long. A feature film screenplay should be between ninety and one hundred thirty pages. The rule of thumb is generally one page equals one minute of screen time. Everyone knows this is not accurate, but it's the closest we have.

(Studios prefer shorter films because exhibitors prefer shorter films because turnover creates action at the popcorn stand and, in case you haven't heard, theatre owners make their real money on concessions, not ticket sales.)

I know some of your favorite films are three hours long, and you have an excuse, your screenplay is an epic. It simply cannot be compressed. This may be the time to address the success factor. . .

It is probably fair to assume that if you are reading this book, you are not yet an established screenwriter. Successful writers do not need my help. Successful writers get hired to write screenplays by producers. When you are trying to break into the business, it is very difficult to do so with an unusual screenplay. I will have more to say about this later when we discuss content. For now, bear in mind that producers hate to read. When a two hundred page manuscript thuds onto their desk, recommended or not, they get very depressed, and unless there is a prominent screenwriter's name on the cover, they groan.

William Goldman says all scripts should be fifteen pages too long, because all producers are going to trim that much regardless of whether your script needs it. You may as well give them a bit of fat to work on or they will eviscerate your masterpiece. This is appropriately cynical and usually true. The need-to-meddle instinct found in producers unequipped to actually write is sky high. But it is also true that Goldman, a super-successful, high-priced, widely admired screenwriter, sends his scripts to people who are going to make his films. You, on the other hand, are sending out your screenplay anywhere you can in the hope that someone will read it and your fortune will be made. To deliberately overwrite by fifteen pages is hardly putting your best foot forward.

I suggest, as it happens, just the opposite. Don't be afraid to underwrite. A good, tight script will result. If the story is good, it will still be there. Then, when the producer finds that it reads like lightening, he will call you in, praise your work, and suggest that one or two things be "fleshed out." Now you go home, pick up the pages you cut, put them back in, and the producer thinks you are an extremely accommodating writer, and that he has been a big help. In the meantime, he is still impressed with the tautness of your writing, because his impression of you is from the first draft.

So Goldman advises a first draft of fifteen extra pages; I advise five or ten too few. Take your pick. But remember, he gets paid in advance.

Don't format your screenplay in 12 characters to the inch pitch.

You will see this from successful writers sometimes. They know they can pack more on a page, and with the luxury of being wanted, they tend to pour everything into the manuscript. However, it is more difficult to read, and gives the impression of an overwritten screenplay, since too many words are going to be packed on the pages.

Ten characters to the inch (a font size of 12 in Courier) is a far better format, standard, and easier to read. It flows with the easy speed of a good movie and the reader turns pages—something readers love to do with rapidity—more often. If you can't fit your screenplay into 90 to 120 pages with this format, your screenplay is overwritten and needs editing anyway.

Font type is always Courier. I have seen a few screenplays in other type fonts, but they tend to look like columns in the newspaper or cue cards for Jay Leno's monologue. Stick with Courier.

Don't make grammatical errors,

I made a concerted effort.

(One person cannot make a group effort.)

syntactical errors,

That is something up with which I will not put.

(Bad syntax really slows the flow of a read.)

or errors of definition.

"Shakes his head" means no. "Nods his head" means yes. In reading a screenplay, I once missed a major plot point because the author had confused the two.

Don't confuse there, their, and they're, or your and you're, it's and its, no, know and now, and etc. If you are not good at stuff like that, get a friend who is to proof your work. Don't rely on spell-checking software programs, because they don't catch things like that. Many readers have a background in English literature and get annoyed at little things (and they are already condescending to read screenplays in order to eat while they write the Great American Novel), so don't annoy them unnecessarily.

Don't make spelling and typo errors.

Have a relyable frend proof read your manuscript for speling and typos. A reader's attention, witch ought to be fokused on your story, is drawn to blunt misteakes. They might not blame you, they might schrug it off as the typists fawlt, but then you have to draw them into your story all over again.

Use a good printer.

If you are still writing on a typewriter, you need the Guild's ageism committee, not this book. Most writers today are taking advantage of modern technology and the miracle of rewrite potential—the personal computer.

Computer users with dot matrix printers will have to upgrade to ink jet or laser.

Here you are, this starving screenwriter who can barely afford to pay the electric bill, scraping your pennies together to buy a computer, and here I am telling you that your printer is too cheap.

This brings us back to the problem of readers having to read a lot. We read fast because if we cannot a screenplay in a single sitting we lose continuity. Anything that makes reading—physically reading—your screenplay easier for us is going to make it easier for you to convince us it is a good story, with *flow* and *rhythm* and *pacing* (and all those things the other books on how to write a screenplay have coached you on), because those things are effected by the reader's ability to read the screenplay *smoothly*. And dot matrix printers are as hard to read as faded photocopies, which you should avoid like the plague, along with an agent who charges you money up front.

Unless you have a quality printer, take your floppy disc to someone who does, and have a decent copy printed out. Sorry, but there it is.

Don't use special, printed covers.

Don't get artsy-craftsy. Don't attempt to do the art work for a screenplay that has yet to be shot. You are a writer. Let your words impress.

Avoid hard covers. Stick with paper. Cardboard is inflexible, and is too difficult to hold in the standard 8-1/2" x 11" manuscript size. Card stock—a heavier weight but still flexible paper—is usually the best choice.

This applies to the binding as well.

Binding ought to be the standard three holes with brads at top and bottom. Special stuff, spiral or glued, special folders, binders, and etc., only annoy readers.

Two-sided

Some of the major agencies are now using both sides of the paper in a noble attempt to combat environmental deterioration (and save on paper bills). This is certainly okay. Think how many more scripts a producer can stuff into his briefcase for the weekend, thinking a thin script will be a light read. But if you are using both sides, you've got to make sure to leave a 1- 1/2" margin on the right side of the odd-numbered pages, and the left side of the even-numbered pages, or the last words of your sentences on the verso will disappear into the binding. (The *verso*, in publishing terms, is the left side, or even-numbered page, of the book. The *recto* is the right side, or odd-numbered page. The things writers pick up.) When computer programs catch up with this recent practice, you'll probably be able to do this automatically. Until then, you might want to put an inch and a half on both sides to be safe.

People don't talk to themselves.

Some do, I suppose. But if so, that is a major characteristic, that needs to be carefully and consistently planted on the character. Nothing is worse in a film than having a character say something to himself that is obviously for the benefit of the audience.

Sometimes they talk to dogs, cats, parrots, mirrors, or photographs, but that is also a special characteristic you should be careful with, because if it looks like an author's excuse to set out some information for the audience, we can tell.

I'm afraid you don't get points for neatness.

But bear in mind that successful screenwriters have secretaries and computers, and you are competing with them. Certainly a great story will shine through typing errors and unfamiliar formats, but why risk anything that s l o u g h s t h e r e e d e r d o w n? Why risk an executive flipping through a couple of pages half-heartedly, spotting inexperience, and not bothering to finish it?

• • •

Those are the basic mechanics. Now for the two major defects I see over and over again: **overwriting** and **lack of clarity**. This is so important, I'll say it again.

OVERWRITING and LACK OF CLARITY

These two common faults have killed more good stories than all the editors in all the news rooms in America. If you can avoid these two **don'ts**, your screenplay can suffer from all the other don'ts in this book, and you might still have a well-written screenplay.

OVERWRITING

Readers often have that "this will never end" feeling, then look up to find themselves on page thirty-five.

On rare occasions, one hundred thirty-five pages have passed before we know it.

In spite of warning you that screenplays should run between ninety and one hundred thirty pages, bear in mind that the real truth about length is not in the page numbers any more than it is in the number of minutes a finished film may be. See *Ben Hur, Lawrence of Arabia* and *The Deerhunter*. See the eight-hour stage production of *Nicholas Nickelby*.

Sustain our interest, and you can have as many pages as you want. If every scene informs and entertains, reads smoothly, moves the plot forward, adds new information, and keeps up the pace, you can probably write two hundred pages for all anyone cares.

Overwriting can generally be spotted on the very first page. It looks something like this.

```
We ZOOM IN on a farmhouse. A quiet, pastoral scene.
Smoke curls from a red-brick chimney, cows laze in
the fields. It is early morning, the sun just
peeking its head over magnificent Iowa mountains in
the distance. A clear, Spring day. White lace
curtains wave gently back and forth through open
windows, where the McCORMACK family sleeps. ROVER,
however, is already nosing about the yard, and a
RED ROOSTER is just trying to decide whether or not
to let loose a blast of the old cock-a-doodle-dos.

                     CUT TO:


MELODY'S WINDOW.

We peek in and see a typical child's bedroom,
country style. Homemade toys and games clutter a
throw rug, overalls and muddy shoes are piled in
the closet. MELODY, a freckle nosed blonde of four-
years-old who would win anybody's heart, is curled
up with a stuffed teddy bear at least her size.
Both wear Dr. Denton's. Other stuffed animals rest
here and there, eyeing the chosen one with
suspicion.
```

Zzzzzzz. . .

We all know what a farmhouse looks like. The production designer is going to put whatever animals he wants in the yard. The movie will shoot during the season the star is available. The lace curtains will be whatever color is hanging in the house the location manager finds conveniently located near a town with reasonable facilities, and anyway, *none of this is as good as our own imagination on Iowa farmhouses.*

Or almost any other place. I suppose if your opening scene is an establishing shot of a small village in Manchuria in 1927 inhabited by yak farmers, you can assume that no one reading your script has any idea what the place looks like. And so, whatever is there that is *vital to the story and tone*, will need to be described.

But **don't write prose.** This is not a novel. Just write

```
EXT. IOWA FARMHOUSE - DAWN

An isolated, working farm, in a magnificent valley
of corn fields.

INT. CHILD'S BEDROOM

MELODY, age 6, freckles and hair the color of the
ripening wheat, is asleep with her favorite stuffed
animal.
```

or something along those lines.

Write the essence of the scene. Write the essence of the shot. Allow for the reader's imagination.

And this is why: because when the reader has to read all that description, page after page, new scene after new scene, action by action, it will slow the story down tremendously.

Of all the items a story must have to successfully enrapture a reader, *pacing* is one of the most important. Although the pacing of your film is ultimately going to be determined in the editing room, the pacing of your screenplay is going to be determined by the way you write; the manner in which you present your story.

Another example of what not to do:

```
INT. NIGHTCLUB - NIGHT

This is a tacky, out of the way place in New Jersey
where they haven't seen enough customers to meet
the rent in years. There is stale smoke drifting in
and out, a tired barmaid murmuring to the owner
behind the bar. You know the kind of place, contact
paper on the piano. Several small tables up front,
around the edge of an even smaller dance floor. One
couple is dancing, but what to, we're not sure.
Probably their own drummer.
```

Too much. Just pick one or two telling details to give your club the right atmosphere. Let the reader imagine the rest:

```
INT. NIGHTCLUB - NIGHT

A run down place in New Jersey, the kind with
contact paper on the piano.
```

Too much description slows down the action. When the film is made, the set will be decorated without your help.

It is especially important not to go into long stage details about the set. This is the second paragraph of the above:

```
On the left, an old juke box. In the back, two pool
tables, their felt long torn. On the right, a long
bar with the owner's only pride and joy, Longhorn
steer antlers over the oversized mirror.
```

"Left" and "right" is for a theatre set. On film, the minute the camera goes for a reverse angle, your whole left and right thing is blown. That must seem very obvious, but I've seen it again and again in submissions from top agencies.

As for the furniture, unless your scene takes place on the planet M-235 and they have a whole different way of living, there is no need to slow your screenplay down with all that setting. (Even the planet M-235 is going to be more in the domain of the production designer, I have to remind you.)

Exceptions? Of course. Some things are *necessary*. An argument taking place in a room in which

```
A gun is on the coffee table.
```

certainly causes suspense.

Here then, is a good rule to follow (like all rules, it's meant to be broken. But like all rules, follow it before you decide that you have good reason to stray): Go through your screenplay. Take every piece of static description, and *reduce it to one sentence*. Work on that sentence until it gives the facts and the image you want. Limit your description of new places to a well chosen phrase.

Add anything vital in the way of props. Emphasis on the word vital. We can assume that an ancient castle has various suits of armor standing around. We *cannot* assume there are golf clubs lying on a tennis court.

Finally, if atmosphere is a key element in your film, a word or two is all right as well. (Some castles are spooky, others are comfortable. Sometimes the rain is a dangerous element, sometimes it isn't.)

When you read it over, try to ascertain if the few lines can be read within about the same amount of time that you expect that particular image to be on the screen. Not in real time, but in relative time. Within, that is, the pacing of your own screenplay. For example, if you want an opening establishing shot to linger on the screen throughout five minutes of credits, you can linger over the description, writing a full paragraph. If a man is running down a short hall, try to say so quickly, because he will probably cover the distance in a hurry. If you want the audience scared out of its wits while he is creeping down the hall, you want to prolong the moment. Do so by stretching out your description a bit so the reader too is in suspense. Always try to add vital new information with each sentence.

Because this is **the most common fault** in screenplays, let's really nail this home:

```
David and Gage shoot pool at a huge mahogany table.
```

Pool tables are regulation size. Although not all are mahogany, the fact that we already know we are in the mansion of a very rich man should tell the designer all he needs to know. Hence

```
David and Gage are shooting pool.
```

—is enough.

Here is the setting of a scene from the middle of a bad screenplay:

```
INT. RESTAURANT - NIGHT

Another restaurant. Which is like cutting from the
BMT local to the Orient Express, and calling it
"another train."

We're at Lutèce, for dinner.
```

FIND Jimmy and Heather at a table for two in one of
the formal upholstered dining rooms upstairs. Both
look splendid, but stiff: Is this a celebration, or
a truce?

He's washing down sautéed sweetbreads with a rare
Chateau Rayas which he refreshes from a carafe.
She's picking at pelerines a la Meridionale, and
sipping ice water.

There is a nervous CLATTERING of silverware in lieu
of conversation. Then—

Enough already. One problem at a time.

INT. RESTAURANT - NIGHT

Another restaurant. Which is like cutting from the
BMT local to the Orient Express, and calling it
"another train."

This kind of prose does not help the reader visualize what is
taking place. Comparisons ("Which is like. . .") and metaphors ("He's
as subtle as a sledgehammer") are for novels. Imagery in a screenplay must be created by brief, clear, direct description. You can not
compete with anyone's imagination.

We're at Lutèce, for dinner.

Why not The Four Seasons? Screenplays can benefit from locale. Naming the restaurant is all right, really. As long as you understand that the scene will probably not be shot there. But there is
no point to naming a specific site *and* describing the whole place.
Either—

INT. LUTECE RESTAURANT - NIGHT

—or—

INT. RESTAURANT - NIGHT

Very expensive and chic.

—would be more than enough.

```
FIND Jimmy and Heather at a table for two in one of
the formal upholstered dining rooms upstairs. Both
look splendid, but stiff: Is this a celebration, or
a truce?
```

I never quite know what FIND means. Are they lost? Does the author want a long, slow PAN through the restaurant until the CAMERA arrives at the subject? Do we start on a painting over their heads and crane down to them? What? If none of the above, then—

```
Jimmy and Heather.
```

—is enough. FIND is fine for a TRACKING SHOT, but it must be clear where the shot originates. Write

```
Hungry diners and busy waiters in a chic, expensive
restaurant, where we

FIND Jimmy and Heather.
```

Furthermore:

```
A table for two.
```

We can assume that if Jimmy and Heather are there, it's a table for two. It's certainly not a table for one, unless someone is standing. **Don't enumerate the obvious** unless something special and unclear is necessary (maybe the table is for four, and they are waiting for another couple).

```
Upstairs.
```

How do we know? Was there an establishing shot of the building? (No.) Did the actors climb a flight of stairs on camera? (No.) As it happens, there are windows in Lutèce's upstairs dining room. But you didn't know that.

```
Splendid, but stiff.
```

All right. They are well dressed and a little nervous. But

```
Is this a celebration, or a truce?
```

Why ask the reader? Rhetorical questions in screenwriting are very dangerous. Don't try to be tantalizing. If they are going to be quiet for a bit, then—

```
(pause)
```

—is probably good enough. Or—

```
They're eating in silence.
```

—might tell us of their awkwardness, but don't ask questions of the reader.

```
He's washing down sautéed sweetbreads with a rare
Chateau Rayas which he refreshes from a carafe.
She's picking at pelerines a la Meridionale, and
sipping ice water.
```

Unless this is going to be a cookbook cleverly disguised as a screenplay, why do we need to know what is being eaten? It is irrelevant to the upcoming scene. (Take my word. I had to read the whole screenplay.)

If he is "Washing down..." he has poor manners. Maybe at a chuck wagon, but in an expensive restaurant? And have you ever had sweetbreads? They're calf pancreas. Yuch.

"Pelerines a la whatever" is lost on me, and if the Chateau Rayas is so rare, why is it served in a carafe rather than poured from the bottle?

But most of all, *who needs a reader thinking all these irrelevant things?* Just tell us what is important to the scene. E.g.–

```
There is a nervous CLATTERING of silverware in lieu
of conversation. Then—
```

Obviously there is an awkwardness. Okay, good, that tells us something about the scene.

So, all we really need here is—

```
INT. LUTECE RESTAURANT - NIGHT

Jimmy and Heather over dinner. There is an
awkwardness in lieu of conversation. Then
```

—and etc.

The reader will assume the normal. Places we know well (an office, a suburban home, McDonald's) need no explanation at all. Describe the abnormal—exotic places or historical periods. For example:

```
OPERATING ROOM - THE LONDON HOSPITAL

We see a bellows pumping air into the open grate of
a cast iron stove. We hear moaning in the
background. The coals flare to a fierce glow. From
the mouth of the stove protrude the handles of
several cauterizing irons, their heads imbedded in
the coals. Up above the irons, Treves stands by a
waist-high operating table covered with black
leather. His face is illuminated by an oil lantern
held by a nurse.

The room is fairly dark owing to the oppressive
overcast sky seen through two windows. There is
also a large sink, a cupboard containing dressings,
gags, manacles, emetics and other unattractive
things, and two hard chairs.

TWO STUDENTS and two other DOCTORS, MR. FOX and MR.
HILL, are present. The two Students are pulling
with constant pressure on a rope tied to the
patient's leg. Treves and Mr. Fox are working on a
chest wound caused by a machine accident. There are
gear-wheel marks getting progressively deeper as
they near a great open gash. Mr. Hill places a
cotton mask over the patient's nose and mouth and
applies drops of subside and he is unconscious. ²⁷
```

Those are three good paragraphs because, (1) they read in about the same time a director should spend on the shots, (2) the period and locale is unusual, and (3) it creates an ambiance of medical horror that is important to the coming story.

Other places need dramatic impact:

```
INT. ALIEN STRUCTURE

They enter the organic labyrinth, playing their
lights over the walls. Revealing a BIO-MECHANICAL
LATTICE, like the marrow of some vast bone. The air
is thick with STEAM. Trickling water. The place
seems almost alive. 28
```

Remember, too, that most readers live in Los Angeles or New York. If your film takes place somewhere fairly exotic (to Angelenos), describe it:

```
THROUGH A WINDSHIELD

We are pulling into the snow swept parking lot of a
one-story brick building. Broken neon at the top of
the building identifies it as the Jolly Troll
Tavern. A troll, also in neon, holds a champagne
glass aloft.


INSIDE

The bar is down scale even for this town. Country
music plays on the jukebox. 29
```

Note the amount of small details in that short description that make for vivid imagery.

Some places are practically plot points. When a mysterious man walks to his home, this author wanted you to see it clearly:

```
MACLEOD'S HOME - 1182 HUDSON STREET, SOHO

Surrounded by Irish bars, art galleries, rubble-
filled lots.

MacLeod heads for a run-down shop next to a
dilapidated ten-story glass-and-iron warehouse.

On the shop door:

R. NASH—ANTIQUES
```

Rummaging for keys, he unlocks the door and goes inside.

CUT TO:

MACLEOD IN A RISING FREIGHT ELEVATOR

The doors open. Before him:

A HUGE, OPEN, NEW YORK LOFT

The change from drab outside to sumptuous inside is stunning. Exotic fish swim in a huge aquarium.

MacLeod descends the stairs to:

A SUNKEN LIVING ROOM

filled with modern art. High ceilings, comfortable sofas, Adam fireplace, spectacular views of the river. Moving past speakers and TVs, he drops his keys on a table beside an intercom and answering machine. In a silver frame on the mantle: a photo of MacLeod with a young girl, 1952. MacLeod moves through:

A GEORGIAN DINING AREA

Queen Anne table, silver candlesticks, tapestries on the wall. He enters:

AN ULTRA-MODERN KITCHEN

Loosening his tie, he fixes a drink and walks out.

CUT TO:

MACLEOD

entering his silver room. Elegant and oval. Fabric walls. Sofas, tables, displays of ancient artifacts: On one wall, like spokes of a wheel: 13 broad swords. Beside them, a bronze shield, claymore and cloak—the black-and-yellow tartan of the Clan MacLeod. Sipping his drink, he sinks into

```
a sofa, eyeing a glass case lit by pin-spots.
Inside:

An ancient sheepskin doll.

A 16th century Catalan feathered hat.

A rusty anvil and tongs.

MacLeod stares at the anvil and tongs, remembering: [30]
```

Not only do we get MacLeod's actions and a description of his elegant loft—which, as a big contrast to the cheesy neighborhood is obviously a character element—but a number of the "props" listed are relevant to upcoming events. And all in a pretty smooth, straightforward sequence.

Here's a set description that tells us a great deal about ambiance and character:

```
Rabin's office can only be described as a disaster
area. The desk is cluttered with weeks, perhaps
months or even years of paperwork that could never
conceivably be sorted out.
    Above his desk is a bulletin board. It is a
breathtaking catastrophe of papers, wanted posters,
rap-sheets, memos and post-its. This is in the
neighborhood of decades. Rabin is a man with a system
so cryptic, so far beyond the comprehension of
others, he himself is most likely baffled by it. [31]
```

This is one of my personal favorites. In Beverly Hills, we arrive at

```
EXT. HOUSE - DAY

It's the kind of house I'm going to buy if this
movie becomes a big hit.
```

(As it happens, the script was Shane Black's *Lethal Weapon.* It should happen to you.)

Now here's an example of the opposite problem. Call it underwriting:

```
INT. CAROL'S ROOM - NIGHT

Carol tosses and turns, unable to sleep.
```

Believe it or not, this is an example of a common error. You can't guess what it is yet, but listen to this:

This is the first time in the screenplay that "Carol" appears.

Got it now? Who the hell is Carol? Boy, girl, man, woman? Old or young? Is her room a dormitory? Is she alone? Whoever she is makes an enormous difference to the scene.

And we have no idea where "Carol" came from. She just popped into the screenplay unaccountably.

In other words, two errors seem to consistently crop up in screenplays. Either the screenwriter over-describes new scenes and characters, wasting an entire paragraph on the furnishings of a room and the color of someone's dress when it hardly matters, or else the screenwriter leaves it out completely.

If this is the first time Carol appears, you need something like:

```
INT. CHILD'S BEDROOM - NIGHT

A 6-year-old tosses and turns.
```

As for her name, slip it in when you can, and when, if possible, the audience is going to hear it for the first time.

The principal task of the screenwriter is to create a vivid series of images, within an acceptable length, that delineate your story through action and description. One way to accomplish this is to find something small but telling, and let the reader's imagination fill in the rest. A house on a hill:

```
It's the most expensive in the city.
```

A restaurant:

```
Filled with trendoids and trendettes.
```

A boat:

```
It isn't going to win any races.
```

A person:

```
He's not the ugliest person in the room, but he's
the most disagreeable.
```

Whenever you think you are pounding out reams of terrific prose, remind yourself that F. Scott Fitzgerald, William Faulkner, Norman Mailer, Truman Capote, Gore Vidal, and a host of other great twentieth century writers all flopped in Hollywood.

One result of overwriting is a reader slogging through your story, saying, "Yeah, yeah, come on already." Another is that too much information is even more confusing than too little and leads the second biggest defect in screenwriting, a

LACK OF CLARITY

```
A cop walks along his beat.
```

What do you see? A policeman in uniform, right? But if I say,

```
A man is a plainclothes cop.
```

What do you see?

Nothing, because if a cop is in plainclothes, how would we know he's a cop?

Here's some interesting dialogue from a recent screenplay:

```
        What in the Ÿ$%@#!Z*! name
        are you doing?
```

How does an actor say that?

Often there is a lack of clarity **in description**, so let's start with one of the worst examples of screenwriting I have ever read:

```
THE BURNS' HOUSE IN S.E. LOS ANGELES - SAME NIGHT

The brothers, BILL & RONNIE BURNS, rent a house
together. BILL is a short, stocky, sloppy guy. He
drinks beer a lot and tends to be a loud mouth.
RONNIE, at 28, is seven years younger. He's a tall,
```

well-built, rough and sexy looking guy. RONNIE is fairly quiet and reads selectively, while BILL never reads at all. RONNIE has always looked up to his older brother, but the last year there's been a growing tension between them. That's when RONNIE started going steadily with LORELEI, who finally left him two months ago, no longer able to tolerate BILL, who continually drove a wedge between RONNIE and herself.

They both work sporadically - BILL on construction and RONNIE as a house painter, handyman. They do a lot of hanging out with their friends who often drop by the "party" house. All these men have low self-esteem. They are frustrated with themselves and society for being "losers," but would never admit this to one another.

RONNIE sits in the funky, disordered living room with a book in his hand and shooting the bull with BUCK, a young black, out-of-work neighbor; LOPEZ, a Chicano from the same area; RICHARD, a 17-year-old runaway whom RONNIE picked-up a few weeks ago and brought home; and DUSTY, another neighbor. The T.V. blares "Three's Company." Sometimes a young white kid from Beverly Hills (son of a doctor) comes down to S.E. L.A. to hang our with them for a few days. They don't like him very much. He's called "HAPPY."

Overwriting! you yell. Correct. But also something else. Listen to this line:

The brothers...rent a house together.

and

They both work sporadically.

How can you film that? **There is virtually nothing in these three paragraphs that belongs in a screenplay, because *none of it can be shot*. How about**

RONNIE is fairly quiet and reads selectively, while BILL never reads at all.

Does this means that the actor playing Ronnie is thumbing through his library, reading every other book, while Bill is staring glassy eyed at the television?

In the first place, all of these characteristics should be developed over the course of the screenplay. Introduce each character as they arrive, or speak, the way the camera will. Even if all these characters are all sitting around in your first establishing shot, just give us the general idea, such as—

```
A pack of good old BOYS, sitting around a low rent
apartment, watching "Three's Company" reruns.
```

—or, if you want a better look—

```
A low rent apartment, where half a dozen men are
watching "Three's Company. The CAMERA PANS slowly
past

BILL BURNS, 35, short, stocky, drinking beer.

His brother RONNIE, 28, tall, well-built, rough and
sexy-looking, in paint-spattered overalls, reading
a paperback.

BUCK, young, black.

LOPEZ, Chicano.
```

—and etc. But **don't** say things like—

```
He lives next door
```

—or—

```
Last year they broke up.
```

How do we know? You can't shoot, "He lives next door." An actor can't act, "Last year they broke up." If there is no way to get the ideas *on screen, in that shot*, then they don't belong in your screenplay.

```
Sometimes a young white kid from Beverly Hills (son
of a doctor) comes down to hang out with them.
```

Is he there now? How do we know he's from Beverly Hills? If he's not there, how do we know he's young? How do we know his father is a doctor?

This is not to strike down the possibility of making some generalized statements. An actor can play adjectives. Clues like "shy," or "nervous," or even "there's a lot of tension between them," can help an actor deliver the lines with the proper subtext, and the reader get the hidden meaning out of them. Check your screenplay for descriptions and generalities, and see if you can't deliver them in a more appropriate form. If your scene—the *action* and the *dialogue*—doesn't convey the appropriate mood, character, history, and hidden motivations of your actors, then the scene is poorly written. If it does, you don't need to explain it in description.

If you must introduce several characters at once, make it *visual*:

```
The Four Bad Men who advance on her are:

1.) the obvious leader, a short, vile, sadistic
German in spectacles by the name of BELZIG.
2.) a trench-coated SECOND NAZI.
3.) a ratty-looking NEPALESE and
4.) a mean MONGOLIAN. The second NAZI and the
MONGOLIAN both carry submachine guns. 32
```

Here is a good intro of seven characters—all principals—who will be going into the jungle on assignment:

```
INT. HELICOPTER - NIGHT

Illuminated by the eerie red glow of NIGHT LIGHTS,
are SEVEN MEN, dressed in jungle camouflage, soft
hats and camouflage face-makeup. They wear no
identity badges or insignias. The men are checking
their WEAPONS, making last minute adjustments to
their GEAR. The compartment reverberates with the
NOISE of the THUMPING ROTORS and the ROAR of air
from the open doors.
```

BLAIN, weapons and ordinance specialist, a
frightening bull of a man, a 240 pound killer,
removes from his shirt pocket a thick PLUG OF
TOBACCO. He looks across at:

MAC, a huge bear of a man, black, holding an M-60
MACHINE GUN. Blain holds out the tobacco to Mac who
refuses with a gentle shake of the head, a knowing
smile, he knows what's coming. Holding the plug
between his teeth Blain yanks free from his
shoulder scabbard a wicked, ten inch COMBAT KNIFE.
Placing the razor sharp blade next to his lips he
slices through the plug as if it were butter. He
chews thoughtfully.

Seated by the open doorway is RAMIREZ, a slight,
angular man, an East L.A. streetwise Chicano.
Adding a final piece of camouflage TAPE to his pack
HARNESS, he looks up and smiles, faking a throw and
bulleting the tape to:

HAWKINS, the radioman and medic, Irish, street-
tough, reading a rolled-up magazine, as if he were
a rush hour commuter. He snags the tape with an
instinctual snap of the wrist, continuing to read
for a moment before looking up, grinning at
Ramirez, his boyish, eager face belying the rugged
professional beneath. He turns his gaze to the man
next to him:

BILLY, the Kit Carson Scout, an American Indian,
proud, stoic, a man of quiet strength and
simplicity, carefully replacing the FIRING
MECHANISM of his M-203, working its action several
times. He looks up with a smile at Hawkins. [33]

Identifying characters

Too many screenwriters throw names and characters at us willy-
nilly. We struggle to sort them out, and none leave an impression.
You do not have to give us a detailed description. The fact is, really
elegant screenwriting appears to have little description. **Don't give
a police-sketch description of every character**. The truth of a

character should leak out, the audience learning more and more from his actions as the character goes through his assigned scenes.

We do have to start somewhere. Many screenplays just list someone's name and then the scene, forgetting that we don't know if the character is a short alien or a statuesque blonde. We need *something* to trigger our imagination, because you want us to visualize the character.

But whatever you tell us, it has to be communicable by camera or actor. Lines like "This is Lisa Feingold's father" are not helpful. How would we know? Is he wearing a sign that says "Lisa's father"? *Anything in description must be visible on the screen.* If the director cannot shoot it, or the actor act it, it doesn't belong in a screenplay. The reader is *trying to visualize a film.* "This is (character name)"— probably the most common sentence in screenwriting—does not tell us anything. You've wasted three precious words, because we can't conjure up a vision from that sentence for the film running in our mind.

Good screenplays tell a reader *only* what the film can tell an audience. **Don't write what can't be photographed.**

Another example:

```
...revealing a beautiful 18-year-old girl we will
come to know later as AMY.
```

There is nothing categorically wrong with this, and it may be easier in the long run to identify a character with a name. But bear in mind our old axiom—the screenplay should tell us what we see. We can't see that this girl's name is Amy. Writing just "a beautiful 18-year-old girl" is more cinematic.

Again:

```
A sinister man stands at the railing looking at
KEVIN. This man is HOWARD POOLE and he is a C.I.A.
agent.
```

Unless he's wearing a name tag that says "Howard Poole—CIA agent," how do we know this? If you can't *see* it on the screen or *hear* it in dialogue, why bother putting it on the page, because as far as your film is concerned, *it doesn't exist.*

```
Rick turns, seeing his friends BRITTANY HARRISON,
BONITA BROWN, and BARRY ADCOCK. Brittany is a
pretty, freckly-faced blonde. Bonita is an
attractive, hip-looking black girl and Barry is
bespectacled, overweight and carries a video camera
with him wherever he goes.
```

Here's what the audience would actually see:

```
Rick turns. Coming toward him are
a pretty, freckly-faced blonde,
an attractive, hip-looking black girl, and
a bespectacled, overweight man carrying a video
camera.
```

Again:

```
THELMA KNUDSEN CATWULLER hates all three of her
names and has been called T.K. ever since she left
home, where she's called SLATS.
```

(That should be easy to photograph.)

```
At an age that finds her poised on the brink of
losing the battle with gravity, she moves with
unconscious grace. Lots of uncolored hair frames
classic features. Coming from stock made from an
indiscriminate mixture so commonly found in the
Midwest, she radiates good breeding, having not
been bred at all.
```

Whew. I *think* this woman is middle-aged, good looking, has broad hips and albino hair. But I could be wrong. Midwesterners seldom come from indiscriminate stock, urban people do. The midwest—clearly this author has never been there—is Gary Cooper country. "Unconscious grace" is a common catch-phrase, so I suppose it has some meaning, but very few people are really graceful. Observe people walking down the street, and after a while you will notice that most of them resemble animated cartoons.

Here is an opening scene between Jack the Ripper and his first victim in the dark alleys of Soho:

FELICITY FAIRWEATHER ambles along the gutter. She
hears FOOTSTEPS behind her, echoing in the deserted
alley. She stops and looks around.

HER POV: she can barely make out JACK THE RIPPER.

She moves on, a little quicker now.

ANGLE JACK. He follows her, sticking to the
shadows.

ANGLE FELICITY. She crosses to a busier
thoroughfare, and hurries through the crowds,
constantly looking back. She's lost him in the
crowd.

She reaches an empty street. She walks to the next
alley, and turns the corner. But

Jack is there.

    Not bad. But this version of the same scene based on the same
classic story is far more indicative of the suspense and mystery
we want:

A VICTORIAN PROSTITUTE ambles along the gutter. She
hears FOOTSTEPS behind her, echoing in the deserted
alley. She stops and looks around.

IN THE SHADOWS, she can barely make out a TALL MAN
IN A CAPE.

She moves on, a little quicker now.

ANGLE THE CAPE. He follows her, sticking to the
shadows.

ANGLE THE HOOKER. She crosses to a busier
thoroughfare, and hurries through the crowds,
constantly looking back. She's lost him in the
crowd.

She reaches an empty street. She walks to the next
alley, and turns the corner. But

THERE'S THE CAPE. [34]

and etc.

Since we haven't met either of these characters yet, the second version has much more mystery to it. This is what we will see, and only what we will see. Later, after we have been introduced to Jack and he strikes again, we can follow him as JACK, or THE RIPPER. But until we can know that, stick to the way it will appear on screen. Same with the girl. If she has been identified in previous scenes, it's all right to use her name. But to pop FELICITY FAIRWEATHER into the screenplay without warning isn't smooth, and to have to write something like—

A VICTORIAN PROSTITUTE, let's call her FELICITY FAIRWEATHER, ambles along the gutter.

—is cumbersome.

Of course, things don't always work out so easily. What do you do, for example, when your film starts with four pages of dialogue between a man and a woman who will be our hero and heroine? If they know each other well, their names may not come up in the dialogue. The audience won't need their names either. But the reader might find it easier.

So if you are going to use this character a great deal, and you find you just have to name him quickly for the sake of simplicity, there are several ways of going about it. One of the easiest and most subtle is to write your description as the audience sees it. Such as–

A small, nervous MAN comes quickly into the cafe, as if running from someone. He approaches the bartender without taking a seat.

—then put his name over his first dialogue:

                    PETER
          Where's Darlene?

The bartender shrugs.

This description gives us the audience POV, but the dialogue marker identifies him as "Peter," which the reader can remember. From then on, you can say

```
PETER looks around again, darts across the room and
hides behind the piano.
```

If you are introducing a major character and there isn't any real mystery about his early appearances, go ahead and give a brief introduction, such as:

```
This is DETECTIVE STONE HART, and a tougher cop you
will never meet. Right now he's trying to get a cup
of coffee at the counter.
```

Here's a good example of breaking the rule successfully:

```
EXT. LA MANCHA PLAINS

Dusty. Flat. Hot enough to bake your brains if
you're not wearing a hat.

A MERCHANT CARAVAN makes rapid progress down the
road.

                    CARAVAN LEADER
          Out of the way there. OUT OF
          THE WAY!

He waves his horse whip at someone. The heaving
animals and the merchandise obscure our view as
they press on

to REVEAL

a painfully thin, BEARDED GENTLEMAN of advancing
years. He carries a cane and a wrapped parcel. And
they've just about mown him over.

He's not wearing a hat.

His name is ALONSO QUIJANA. He is a country squire
of 50 in the year 1605 in the La Mancha district of
Spain. At that time and place fifty years seems
somewhat older.³⁵
```

The "his name is ALONSO QUIJANA" line is exactly what I warned you about. But bear in mind that (1) this is our star. He's going to be in every scene. And (2) the reader knows by the title that this is a film adaptation of *Don Quixote de La Mancha* by Miguel de Cervantes, and they're expecting to see the old man soon. Finally, (3) the author has already given the reader a very good image with the preceding paragraph. Now putting a name on him isn't done instead of, but in addition to, our first visual image.

But **don't** do this unless the characters are going to be a major or central part of your story, **don't** do it if you want to maintain some mystery about a character's first appearance, and **don't** do it with more than one or two major characters per screenplay if you can help it.

Here's a now famous intro of an eponymous leading character:

```
SLOW PAN as the sound of stray electrical CRACKLING
subsides. FRAME comes to rest on the figure of a
NAKED MAN kneeling, faced away, in the previously
empty yard. He stands, slowly. The man is in his
late thirties, tall and powerfully built, moving
with graceful precision.

C.U. - MAN, his facial features reiterate the power
of his body and are dominated by the eyes, which
are intense, blue and depthless. His hair is
military short.

This man is the TERMINATOR.

He glances down, taking calm inventory of himself,
and notices that a fine white ash covers his skin.
He brushes at it unconcernedly as he walks toward
the fence, scanning his surroundings. ³⁶
```

A good entrance is always a good idea, especially if you hope to snag a star. This is the introduction for a now classic character:

```
          WOMAN
     Will you ask Rick if he'll
     have a drink with us?


          CARL
     Madame, he never drinks with
     customers. Never. I have
     never seen him.
```

>   2ND WOMAN
> What makes saloon-keepers so
> snobbish?
>
>   MAN
> Perhaps if you told him I
> ran the second largest
> banking house in Amsterdam.
>
>   CARL
> The second largest? That
> wouldn't impress Rick. The
> leading banker in Amsterdam
> is now the pastry chef in
> our kitchen...

Nice foreshadowing. And then:

The overseer walks up to a table with a paper in his
hand. In the foreground at the table we see a drink
and a man's hand. The overseer places a check on the
table. The man's hand picks up the check and writes
on it, in pencil: "Okay - Rick." The overseer takes
the check. The camera pulls back to reveal Rick,
sitting at a table alone playing solitary chess.
There is no expression on his face. [37]

For supporting characters, try to keep it simple. There is nothing more confusing than a paragraph such as:

Behind him sit WILSON and GARRISON. Wilson and
Garrison are political operatives who work out of
Sammy's office. Wilson, 28, is tall, blonde,
energetic and wears glasses. He will be the
campaign coordinator. Garrison is 49, gray-haired,
with a cock-eyed, mean stare—a professional
pollster and a cynic. Opposite them, on a couch,
sit Sammy and HELENA. Helena is 38, black; she
dresses like a stylish librarian. She is the
administrator of Sammy's think tank and will be the
Issue's coordinator for the campaign. Throughout
the following scenes...

Too much. Three new characters, all relatively minor as it happens. We'll never keep track of them.

(And of course, you already know that "He will be the campaign coordinator," and "She is the administrator of. . ." can't be filmed and thus tells us nothing.) Also be careful of misusing "blond/blonde." Blond is male, blonde is female. That mistake told me Wilson was a woman, then a man. Lack of clarity.

The above paragraph would have been much simpler and better written as:

```
POLITICAL OPERATIVES sit around, attentive to
Sammy.
```

and then introducing each one as—and if—necessary, when they have their first line of dialogue.

As for minor characters, even a one line part needs some identification.

```
Even his handkerchief is pressed.
```

However, **don't give the full name and description of a very minor, non-plot character** who will disappear before the end of the page. It leads us to believe we need to remember this person, when we don't. A long description of a character only to discover that he's a bit player is misleading. Since you have even less time to identify walk-ons, focus on one or two traits that tell us their general category:

```
...two men on snowshoes. The big one is LITTLE BILL
DAGGETT and he is very big, wrapped in a huge
bearskin robe.
```

```
The smaller one is CLYDE LEDBETTER who isn't small
though he has only one arm.[38]
```

Not likely we'll forget them.

Look at all your character descriptions. The amount of material dedicated to the star, major, supporting, minor, and bit roles should be in proportion to their importance. Use an entire paragraph to describe a character who is going to dominate the story, be in every scene, require a name actor, and be available for sequels.

Otherwise, limit yourself to a sentence or two. Work on establishing character through that character's dialogue and actions.

```
At the COFFEE MACHINE Mike finds DONNA DEMARKO,
glasses, 31, bookish, quiet, an NTSB computer
specialist, with a PhD in Aircraft Engineering, and
STEVE BROWN, 45, charming, funny, an NTSB Flight
Systems Specialist and former Fighter Pilot.
```

Though these two new characters seem to have remarkable resumes, how the hell do we know these things about them? We don't. Neither will the audience. Therefore, if you want the audience to know these things, you're going to have to put it into dialogue. If it doesn't matter, you don't need it in description. You might argue that description like this is part of a character's background, which it is helpful for an actor to know. Maybe. But how does an actor play "Flight Systems Specialist" or "former Fighter Pilot." As for Steve being charming and funny, if you haven't written charming and funny dialogue, he's not, and if you have, you won't need it in the description. Also, capitalizing COFFEE MACHINE is absurd, and capitalizing "Aircraft Engineering" and "Fighter Pilot" is grammatically incorrect.

Okay, time for a quiz. What's wrong with this paragraph?

```
COMMANDER JOHN ADAMS, in his place at the center of
the bridge, studies the instruments on the curved
console in front of him. Adams, young, with rugged
good looks, is dedicated to his crew and ship.
Bold, decisive, he prefers space to his
deteriorating home planet Earth. JUNO FARMAN, the
astrogator, sits to his right at the console with
the tri-dimensional PENROSE CONFORMAL SPACE MAP
behind her. She's beautiful, cold, and ambitious.
At 22 she's already Adams' second in command. To
Adam's left in the Chief Engineer's position sits
ELEANOR QUINN, his former teacher at the Space
Academy and a good friend. No one else would give
the old lady of 43, who has years of space travel
experience behind her, another chance at a voyage
to the stars. She's in charge of the NEUTRINO RADAR
for observation of objects up to interstellar
distances.
```

The answers:

```
Young, with rugged good looks.
```

Not so bad, but a bit of a cliché, don't you think? Every actor in Hollywood has rugged good looks.

```
...is dedicated to his crew and ship.
```

That's a good characteristic, but he can't demonstrate much of that loyalty sitting in his captain's chair. Remind yourself to write in actions that illustrate his dedication, then cut it from the description.

```
Bold, decisive...
```

Likewise .

```
...he prefers space to his deteriorating home
planet Earth.
```

That's his choice, I suppose, though mere pollution might seem pretty good compared to space, where breathing at all is tricky. Nevertheless, if this is an important component of Adams' character, he will have to say so. Write a scene making this clear, and you won't need the description.

```
...the astrogator...
```

I suppose that's a Navigator-to-the-Stars, but we won't know that from where she sits.

```
She's beautiful, cold, ambitious.
```

Okay on the "beautiful," though again you haven't really separated her from any other character in film history except maybe the Wicked Witch of the West, but neither "cold" nor "ambitious" are of any use in description. Write her actions and dialogue as cold and ambitious.

```
...she's Adams' second in command.
```

I hate to be redundant, but I want this point clear: HOW DO WE KNOW? Probably it will be clear as the action unfolds. Make sure it is, and cut it here.

```
...In the Chief Engineer's position...
```

Unless your reader is familiar with the layout of the bridge of a starship in the 25th century, this isn't telling us much.

```
...his former teacher at the Space Academy and a
good friend. No one else would give the old lady of
43, who has years of space travel experience behind
her, another chance at a voyage to the stars.
```

You get it by now. This sounds like she will be an interesting character. Ageism in the space program. The Captain who now has to give orders to his mentor. Write these ideas on your index cards, pin them up under characters, and make sure they get expressed in scenes to follow. Don't express them in prose descriptions.

```
She's in charge of the NEUTRINO RADAR for
observation of objects up to interstellar
distances.
```

We don't really care what she's in charge of. What is she *doing* with the Radar?

In other words, that whole paragraph told us almost nothing cinematically useful.

Two more to look at. . .

```
LIZZIE TABNER punches a few buttons on a keyboard.
She is almost thirty. On the mousy side, but still
attractive. Appealing in a subtle way. Obviously
intelligent and experienced. Exudes confidence.
```

"On the mousy side, but still attractive" is vague, and an obvious attempt to create a not-so-beautiful character without insulting the actress you want to play her. "Appealing in a subtle way," is also vague, and tells us nothing. "Obviously intelligent" and "exudes confidence" are characteristics that need to be written into the dialogue and actions of the character. Likewise, "experienced." At what?

```
...losing his hair.
```

You can't photograph a man losing his hair, unless you have a scene where his hair is dropping out. I believe the author means thin hair. "Balding" is a common word for this, but you won't find it in a dictionary because one is either bald or not.

Lack of clarity in camera work

```
CAMERA VEERS away from him, toward the rear rest
room corridor, through an archway. RASP of a DOOR
sliding shut on metal runners. Sudden TILT as
CAMERA SWINGS around a PHONE BOOTH, into the men's
room foyer. Ahead, a mirror over the sinks. CAMERA
DIAGONALS for it. Several feet away, it STOPS.
```

I guess the simplest thing to say about this example is, *I haven't the faintest idea what is going on here.*

When all is said and done (or overdone in this case) nothing has really happened. The story has moved forward exactly not at all. I suppose the shot is some kind of POV and a man is actually walking into the bathroom and sees whatever is coming up, but I can't be sure. That screenplay was filled with the camera wandering, veering and careening around by itself.

If the CAMERA is doing something, then you're drawing our attention to the camera itself, not to the shot. In the paragraph above I didn't see the shot (I don't think I could have figured it out anyway). I saw the camera, a big old piece of equipment, probably with Panavision stenciled on the side, rolling along like some sort of robot. Surely that is not what the author intended.

The camera should be the *least intrusive* item in a screenplay. And in a film. You don't want an audience to leave a movie saying, "Boy, that camera must have been rolling right alongside that car. It must have been going one hundred miles an hour."

So **don't put in a lot of gratuitous camera instruction**. This can be established easily enough. Just drop it and see if your story still reads smoothly. As long as the content of the shot is clear, you've said enough. The director is going to choose all the angles, lenses, zooms, pans, wipes, cuts, fades, dissolves, tracks, cranes, tilts, and dollies (not to mention veers and diagonals, whatever they are) for the picture. Any camera instructions you have written in—and here's the thing to remember when you're writing them—are only for the *clarity of the story* for the reader's sake. If what you really want to do is direct—and I've yet to meet anyone in Hollywood who doesn't—fine, good luck. But **don't direct when you write**.

I said a screenplay is a blueprint for a film, but maybe we should refine that now. It's an *artist's rendering*. Each sequence must be visually clear to the reader. What is happening on the screen at that moment? Then what? And then? This does not include *how* it is shot, only *what* is shot.

If a character is to be seen staring at someone, then—

```
He hides behind a door, peeking at...
```

—is enough. If his expression is your principal desire, then:

```
CU: a MAN'S face in the shadows, staring intently
at...
```

is fine. But:

```
The CAMERA dollies down a long hall, comes to rest
at a door. We see that it is cracked open and a man
is staring intently out. ZOOM IN on his face,
gazing on...
```

is way too much.

Don't overuse a moving camera. The reader can't keep up with it. If we are in a parked car, just say so. If the car is racing down the highway, say that too. If the director wants to follow it with a camera car alongside, or place his camera on the corner and watch it go by, or in a helicopter overhead, or inside the traveling car, he will. You can't dictate that and by including it in the screenplay you are only distracting from your story.

On rare occasions, I will condone your moving the camera. Again, the only good rule is CLARITY. Have a good reason, and make the shot clear. For example:

```
CAMERA moves slowly up the side of the Empire state
building. At the top, one big ape, hanging on for
dear life.
```

That tells us what that shot is. It is also the audience POV. If you want a character's POV, write:

```
She looks up.

HER POV: The Empire State building, towering
overhead. And finally, at the top, the big guy.
```

As far as special work, such as "hand held," use it sparingly. If you want to show the point of view of a man drunk, or stumbling, or if you want the feeling of one of those six o'clock news flashes, then:

```
HANDHELD SHOT
```

is all right. Screenplay readers can imagine that unsteady, newsreel photography. But it isn't necessary. If your character is drunk, just write the scene and let the director and DP interpret it.

When you must write about the camera, **don't change your point of view in mid-paragraph.**

```
CAMERA PANS slowly along the ridge. It comes to
rest on a smoking barn. We see Indians circling it.
```

For one thing, that says that Indians are circling the camera, not the barn. Use either "We" or the "Camera." You might employ both in a single screenplay without confusing us, but not in a single description. (And don't overdo the "we" stuff. It gets to be a little pretentious. We might not be amused, if you catch our drift.)

```
A bus travels across the George Washington Bridge
toward the CAMERA. The CAMERA is high, catching the
bridge, the Hudson and the City of New York in the
background. The bus is moving toward New Jersey. It
passes through the tollbooth.
```

The first sentence describes a shot. Then, with the second sentence, the author says, nope, that's not the shot, this is the shot. Confusing. If you want a particular angle, say so *before* you describe it. Once you've described something, the reader has seen it for himself. This would have been better:

HIGH ANGLE: The George Washington Bridge over the Hudson River, and the City of New York in the background. A bus is moving toward Jersey. It passes through the tollbooth.

Moreover, if you don't really need the angle, leave it to the reader's imagination (and the director's skill):

EXT. GEORGE WASHINGTON BRIDGE - DAY

A bus is moving from New York to New Jersey. It passes through the tollbooth.

In any case, if you want to use the angle—and **don't use angles often**—use it first, to establish the point of view right away.

Compare these four ways of saying the same thing:

1. WE see a GIRAFFE walk down the street.

2. CAMERA FOLLOWS a GIRAFFE as he walks down the street.

3. ANGLE A GIRAFFE, as he walks down the street.

4. A GIRAFFE walks down the street.

Don't you think #4 is the best?

I once read an opening sequence that was two pages long, followed by:

All from the POV of...

It was a little late to tell us.

Think visually. SEE your scene from the best angle. Without using camera talk, describe what you see:

```
The building looms hundreds of stories over us.

He ties his shoes, while sneaking a look at her.
She's imposing, a breathtaking ten.

Through binoculars, she sees...
```

You do have to establish basic shots. You have to make sure the reader can follow the action like frames of a cartoon, each one individually.

This author has described what he wants us to *know*, rather than *see:*

```
LLOYD and DOWD are in their room, on the second
floor, with Dowd peeking out the door to look at
that same man (a Cop in plain clothes) he pointed
to at the bar a little earlier. The Cop is seated
in a chair in the hallway, right next to the stairs
- the only other exit is in the back way (fire
escape) which is on past him at the end of the
hall. There is no way Lloyd and Dowd can get out of
their room and down either set of stairs without
the Cop knowing.
```

How do we know their room is on the second floor?

If we see Dowd peeking out the door, how do we know what he is looking at?

How do we know the man in plain clothes is a cop? Is he wearing a badge? Not if he's in plain clothes.

How do we know the only other exit is the fire escape? Just because we see two exits being blocked by the man sitting in the chair, how do we know there aren't other exits at the other end of the hall? Or other exits from the room?

Let's go over this example in detail.

```
The room is on the second floor.
```

We see this all the time in screenplays. Worse:

```
This is a big house with six bedrooms.
```

Does this mean a SLOW PAN through all the hallways? Do you expect the audience to count as we go? If there is an establishing shot from outside, how do we know what's inside? If it is not vital that the room is on the second floor, don't waste time telling us. If it is vital, establish it legitimately. Maybe they walked to their room and it was one flight up from the street entrance. Maybe there is a POV shot out a window, or a remark by a character. But if you need us to know that, we have to see it, not be told it in stage directions.

```
Dowd peeking out the door to look at that same
man...
```

Don't describe a man and what he sees at the same time. Write

```
DOWD is peeking out the door.
```

and then

```
HIS POV: A MAN sits at the end of a long hall.
```

It's important to know which shot comes first, the action or the reaction. Compare the above with:

```
A MAN sits at the end of a long hall.

A door at the near end cracks open and DOWD peeks
out at him.
```

The rule: **Don't *tell* us what we need to know, *show* us what we need to know**.

```
The only other exit is in the back (the fire
escape).
```

If we can't see both ends of the hall, we aren't going to know that we are looking at the only way out. **We don't know what we can't see**.

Assuming the screenplay has by now made it quite clear that Lloyd and Dowd would like to get out of the room unobserved, write:

```
DOWD peeks out, looks down the hall.
HIS POV: No exit.
He looks the other way.
A MAN sits guarding the stairs.
```

You can shorten this with something like—

```
DOWD peeks out: No exit one way, a COP the other.
```

—or anything similar, so long as it's linear, by which I mean, one shot/idea (DOWD peeks out), then the next (No exit), and the next (A COP guards. . .).

•   •   •

Longer action sequences need just as much care. The reader must be able to keep track of what is going on, action by action.

Starting on the simplest level, there is nothing wrong with writing:

```
They fight.
```

Stunt men are going to stage the fight, and the director and cinematographer are going to photograph it. You don't need to go into a long explanation, except for those items which are important to your fight and unique to these events.

A long descriptive passage—or a shot by shot breakdown—of the fight, such as–

```
Mike throws a right. Ike blocks it, counters with a
left. Mike goes down, Ike falls on top of him. They
roll to the right, under the table. Ike grabs the
chair and smashes it down, but Mike has rolled out
of the way...
```

—is not really going to help. I'll tell you a secret. The reader is going to skim it, looking for who wins. Because the reader knows perfectly well that the fight probably isn't going to follow your instructions. Having read so many scenes of this kind, the reader gets so he can smell when you're writing something unimportant. He runs his eyes forward, seeking specific information that might change the plot, or tell something of the characters.

Write, then, only what pertains to what is necessary *in the fight*, to *tell your story*, to separate it from all other "they fight's."

One way is to give us the essence of the fight, just as you would write the plot of a ballet, and let the choreographer interpret that.

```
Mike gets an early advantage, and appears to beat
the shit out of Ike.
But Ike's superior footwork and his ability to take
a punch starts to pay off.
Finally Mike gets sloppy and Ike closes for the
advantage...
```

Anything that is taking place, the camera can cover. Anything that just *is*, the camera cannot cover.

Here is a big battle between two armies, not at all overwritten:

```
THE BATTLE OF LOCH SHIEL, 1536

MacLeods and Frazers collide in fury. Raging
carnage. Fog slowly moving in.

MacLeod, Dugal and Angus in the thick of it.
MacLeod tries to engage the enemy. Each time they
avoid him.

Dugal's helpless beneath three Frazers. Flying from
the saddle, Angus kills two of them. The third
bolts.

Gradually, the fog makes it impossible to see more
than a few yards. Each man's battle is his own,
hopelessly separated from the battling clansmen
around them. 39
```

That gives us the basics, and the director and his stunt coordinator can do a lot with it. The fog and the visibility offer a marvelous image about the loneliness of this kind of warfare.

Next we have a battle scene from a film in which, like many films, there are several action scenes, and thus each action sequence has to have a unique identity, or they will become repetitive. In this scene the Scots surprise the English with their tactical ability.

LORD TALMADGE, AT HIS COMMAND POST

The husky English commander's blood boils from
Cheltham's report. Before he can respond, they see
WALLACE'S SPEARMEN taking up a position on the far
side of the bridge. Suddenly the Scots turn and
lift their kilts and moon the English!

>   TALMADGE
>   Insolent bastards! Full
>   attack! Give no quarter! And
>   I want this Wallace's heart
>   brought to me on a plate!

Cheltham spurs his horse to form up the attack...

EXT. THE FIELD BELOW STIRLING CASTLE - DAY

The English army moves forward toward the bridge.
It's so narrow that only a single file of riders
can move across it at any one time. The English
heavy cavalry, two hundred knights, cross
uncontested, and form up on the other side.

WITH WALLACE AND THE SCOTS

Things look terrible. Stephen turns to William.

>   STEPHEN
>   The Lord tells me He can get
>   me out of this mess. But
>   he's pretty sure you're
>   fooked.

ON THE ENGLISH SIDE

Talmadge sees the Scots doing nothing.

>   TALMADGE
>   Amateurs! They do not even
>   contest us! Send across the
>   infantry.

> GENERAL
> M'Lord, the bridge is so
> narrow -

> TALMADGE
> The Scots just stand in
> their formations! Our
> cavalry will ride them down
> like grass. Get the infantry
> across so they can finish
> the slaughter!

The English leaders shout orders and keep their men moving across the bridge. Talmadge gestures for the attack flag.

THE CAVALRY ON THE OTHER SIDE OF THE BRIDGE

The English knights see the signal banners, telling them to attack. They take the lances from their squires, and lower the visors of their helmets. Proud, plumed, glimmering; they look invincible. Their huge horses, themselves draped in scarlet and purple, look like tanks. The knights charge!

Their hooves thunder; the horses are so heavy the ground literally shakes with the charge.

The Scots stand and watch them come on. It's difficult to imagine the courage this takes; from the POV OF THE SCOTTISH LINES we see the massive horses boring in...we feel the RISING THUNDER of the charge, closer, closer...

Wallace moves to the front of the lead group of Scots.

> WALLACE
> Steady! Hold...hold
> ...Now!

The Scots snap their 14 foot spears straight up in unison.

> WALLACE
>>> Form!

Now the spearmen snap the spears forward in ranks, the first line of men bracing their spears at an angle three feet above the ground, the men behind them bracing theirs at a five foot level, the men behind that bracing at seven feet.

The English knights have never seen such a formation. Their lances are useless and it's too late to stop! The momentum that was to carry the horses smashing through the men on foot now becomes suicidal force; knights and horses impale themselves on the long spears like beef on skewers.

TALMADGE

can see it; but worse is the sound, the SCREAMS OF DYING MEN AND HORSES, carried to him ACROSS THE BATTLEFIELD.

WALLACE AND HIS MEN

are protected, behind a literal wall of fallen charges and knights. Wallace draws his broadsword and leads his swordsmen out onto the field, attacking the knights that are still alive. Most are off their horses; a few have managed to pull up their mounts. Wallace and his men are so much more mobile than the armored knights that it's no contest; they hack through the knights; the field runs with blood. Wallace faces Talmadge in the distance.

>>> WALLACE
>>> Here I am, English coward!
>>> Come and get me!

TALMADGE is even more enraged—and his judgment is gone.

>>> TALMADGE
>>> Press the men across!

                    CHELTHAM
          But M'Lord!

Talmadge himself gallops forward.

                    TALMADGE
          PRESS THEM!

WALLACE smiles. He grabs Hamish.

                    WALLACE
          Tell Mornay to ride to the
          flank and cross upstream.
          Wait! Tell him to be sure
          the English see him ride
          away!

Hamish hurries off with the message.

The English infantry keeps moving across the little
bridge.

The Scottish nobles watch from their positions on
horseback. They have a few dozen mounted riders,
none heavily armored.

                    LOCHLAN
          If he waits much longer—

Hamish hurries up.

                    HAMISH
          Ride around and ford behind
          them!

                    MORNAY
          We should not divide our
          forces!

                    HAMISH
          Wallace says do it! And he
          says for you to let the
          English see you!

                    MORNAY
               (understanding)
          They shall think we run
          away.

Mornay leads his riders away.

LORD TALMADGE

sees the Scottish nobles ride off, and shouts to
Cheltham...

                    TALMADGE
          See! Every Scot with a horse
          is fleeing! Hurry! Hurry!

He drives half his army across the river.

WALLACE

lifts his sword.

                    WALLACE
          For Scotland!

He charges down the hill...

THE FIGHT AT STIRLING BRIDGE - VARIOUS SHOTS

The Scots follow Wallace on foot, charging into the
English.

The English leaders are stunned by the ferocious
attack.

                    TALMADGE
          Press reinforcements across!

The English leaders try to herd more of their foot
soldiers onto the bridge, which only jams them up.
Meanwhile, on the other side of the bridge, Wallace
and his charging men slam into the English infantry
with wild fury. The English fall back on each
other, further blocking the bridge.

UP ON THE HILLTOP

The nobles look back with grudging admiration.

>   MORNAY
>   He's taking the bloody
>   bridge! The English can't
>   get across! He's evened the
>   odds at one stroke!

With rising desire to join the bandwagon, the
nobles spur...

DOWN ON THE PLAIN, Wallace and the attacking men
drive the English back, killing as they go. The
Scots reach the bridge itself. The waters below it
run red with blood.

Talmadge has begun to panic.

>   TALMADGE
>   Use the archers!

>   GENERAL
>   They're too close, we'll
>   shoot our own men!

ON THE BRIDGE

The Scots are carving their way through the English
soldiers; nothing can stop them. Wallace is
relentless; each time he swings, a head flies, or
an arm. Hamish and Stephen fight beside him,
swinging the broadsword with both hands. Old
Campbell loses his shield in the grappling; an
English swordsman whacks at him and takes off his
left hand, but Campbell battles him to the ground
with his right, and stabs him. Reaching the English
side of the bridge, the Scots begin to build a
barrier with the dead bodies.

The English are not without courage. Cheltham leads
a desperate counterattack. The Scots make an
impenetrable barrier of slashing blades. Still

Cheltham keeps coming; Wallace hits him with a vertical slash that parts his helmet, his hair, and his brain.

Talmadge has seen enough; he gallops away. The remaining English general tries to save the army.

> GENERAL
> We are still five thousand!
> Rally!

The English try to form up; but the Scottish horsemen, fording the river high upstream, come crashing into the English flank and ride at the surprised infantry.

AT THE BRIDGE, WALLACE

sees the Scottish nobles attacking. The English soldiers are in utter panic, running and being cut down on all sides.

And the Scottish soldiers taste something Scots have not tasted for a hundred years: victory. Even while finishing off the last of the English soldiers, they begin their high-low chant...Even the noblemen take up the chant!

Wallace looks around at the aftermath of the battle; bodies on the field; soldiers lying impaled; stacks of bodies on the bridge; the bridge slick with blood.

Before it can all sink in, William is lifted onto the shoulders of the men.

> SCOTTISH SOLDIERS
> Wal-lace! Wal-lace!
> Wal-lace! [40]

•　•　•

What have we got so far?

Write action. Write reaction. Write dialogue.

Do not write ideas and metaphors.

Write what we are to see on the screen. Write in one sentence or group of sentences together, only what we can see on the screen at one time, or a sequence of actions which we can see on the screen in the order you put them down, one after the other. **Do not write into any one sentence a number of different actions. Do not write what cannot be specifically visualized.**

Here's another well-written, action-filled, suspenseful scene:

```
EXT. ROOF - ON MCCLANE - NIGHT

running for his life, from Fritz and Franco,
doesn't realize he is being herded around the
building toward Karl. Suddenly McClane turns a
corner and sees Karl. The big man fires a burst and
McClane ducks back stopping at the exterior door to
the pump room he used before. It is locked from the
inside.

He BLOWS the lock off with a burst from his machine
gun and slips into the darkness of the:

ELEVATOR SHAFT NEAR PUMP ROOM

Coming quickly out of the pump room, McClane picks
his way over the same ground as a few minutes
before and opens the door to the elevator shaft.
The dimly lit shaft yawns before him. He starts
down the ladder back to the catwalk, moves along
it—STOPS.

The catwalk ends, and the elevator is gone.

INT. PUMP ROOM - OTHER END

Karl crosses, starts to open the door to the
elevator shaft when suddenly their radio crackles
with —

                    HANS' VOICE
            Karl? Franco? Did you catch
            him?
```

> FRANCO
> No, but he's in the elevator
> shaft.

> HANS' VOICE
> Perfect. The elevators are
> locked off. He can't escape.
> Just shut him in and return
> to base.

> KARL
> Hans, he killed my brother —

> HANS
> (more firmly)
> Karl, I know you want him,
> but the police are probably
> on their way. Maybe we can
> convince them it was all a
> mistake, but not if they
> hear gunshots! If you lock
> him in he'll be neutralized—
> now do it! Karl? Karl!

Karl turns off his radio. In the light of their
flashlights, the two other terrorists look at Karl
in stunned disbelief. He opens the door to the
elevator shaft.

INT. ELEVATOR SHAFT - ON MCCLANE

He's OVERHEARD enough of this to realize he's in
deep shit. He backtracks to the air shaft door,
strikes a cigarette lighter.

ELEVATOR SHAFT (OPPOSITE SIDE)

Karl steps off the ladder to the catwalk, his own
gun held ready.

MCCLANE

HEARING Karl's approach, McClane thinks fast, looks
down at his narrow confines, and then at:

HIS WEAPON

and its canvas gunsling and metal strap slides.

BACK TO SCENE

Quickly, McClane lets out all the slack in the
sling. Then, he BRACES the weapon across the
outside opening of the air shaft door and lowers
himself into the:

AIR SHAFT

meanwhile holding onto the canvas sling with his
elbows bent over it like a kid doing a half-assed
skin-the-cat on a swing set.

His feet slowly move down the smooth aluminum walls
until they reach the top of the air duct, then
DANGLE in the open space. He straightens his arms
to give him length enough to touch the bottom edge
of the duct.

Suddenly he FEELS something GIVE above him and
looks up.

CLOSE ON THE SLING

It was designed to carry a gun on a man, not vice
versa. The few inches of extra canvas are sliding
through the clips. When they're gone...he will be
too.

KARL

He moves silently toward the corner.

CLOSE - MCCLANE'S TOES

now only inches from the bottom edge. McClane's
arms are fully extended now. He hears Karl on the
metal catwalk. His muscles strain and quiver.

THE SLING

One of the canvas end slips through the clip.

ON MCCLANE

FALLING. He grabs the ledge of the air duct as he falls and his body slams into the aluminum wall with an echoing BOOM. Above him on the catwalk the rifle rattles on the metal outside the door.

ON KARL

Around the corner Karl FREEZES, unsure of the sound:

ON MCCLANE

holding onto the ledge by his hands. With every ounce of strength he tries to pull himself up into the horizontal duct, clawing for a hold.

ON KARL

He rounds the corner and sees McClane's rifle lying beneath the doorway. He moves to the small door, shines his light and aims his rifle down into the air shaft ready to fire.

HIS P.O.V.

The shaft is deserted. Moving his light around he sees the air duct. Without hesitation he turns and backtracks to the pump room door.

INT. AIR CONDITIONING DUCT - ON MCCLANE - SAME

He lies exhausted and motionless in the narrow crawl space. He awkwardly fishes out the lighter from his shirt pocket and thumbs it ON.

The flickering GLOW shows him this ain't no place for claustrophobics—it's a long, dark and narrow corridor full of weird shadows. The far end (if there even is one?) is BLACK.

```
        MCCLANE
    Whew...for a moment there I
    was worried.
```

He turns out his lighter, and starts crawling. [41]

Nice.

•   •   •

Lack of clarity in writing

He looks like Bogart, down and out in Tampico, in
Treasure of the Sierra Madre, but the shot is pure
High Noon.

Showing off your knowledge of film is usually boring, and very
few Hollywood executives actually know film really well.

```
INT. ELEVATOR - DAY

Loaded to less than capacity, Steven and Harry
stand side by side without speaking.
```

This writer probably meant that Steven and Harry are standing
in an elevator that's crowded but not packed. But what he actually
wrote is that Steven and Harry are drunk, but could get drunker.

For some reason things like this surface often in screenplays.
Maybe because a good editor and copy editor haven't gone over
your writing as they would for a published novel. **Don't assume
that if it's clear to you, it's clear to us.** Ask your friends to read it,
and listen to their advice. And remember that old proverb: If five
people are telling you you're drunk, lie down.

During your polish, read your screenplay with an eye for clarity. Watch for convoluted sentences that may have more than one
meaning:

```
David and Diana stand beside David's old clunker,
now held together with spit and chewing gum,
looking at the building. David's face is lit with
excitement, he gestures with his hands.
```

(1) According to this, the Clunker is looking at the building.

(2) That David's face is lit with excitement is okay, but leave his gestures to the actor.

(3) In describing the car, "old clunker" is sufficient. Unless you want shots of spit and chewing gum, the rest is unnecessary .

Also from that screenplay is:

```
The furniture is handmade by David.
```

Sounds like he's a good carpenter, but *how do we know?*

Here is what ought to be a suspenseful sequence—two suspicious men following a third—but is instead a hopelessly muddled paragraph.

```
INT. AN INN IN BALTIMORE - 1849

Philip checks into an Inn and promptly deposits his
bag in his room. This catches the eye of two
suspicious looking men, one of whom takes a seat at
the bar. Philip enters the bar-room.
```

There are a dozen scenes in this short description. At the check-in desk, up the elevator, down the hall, in the hotel room, back in the bar as he enters, etc. etc. etc. In writing action, you have to write what happens on a step by step basis, because that's what we need to see. Let's rewrite this sequence:

```
INT. AN INN IN BALTIMORE - 1849

Philip enters the lobby and approaches the desk. As
he registers...

Two men watch him from behind newspapers they
pretend to read.

Philip goes

UPSTAIRS

following the bellboy. They enter
```

A ROOM

where Philip tips the bellboy. After he leaves,
Philip returns

DOWNSTAIRS

and crosses to the bar. As he goes to the counter,
we notice

One of the men from the lobby has taken up a seat
in the back of the bar, and is still watching
Philip.

I haven't altered or rewritten the film one bit. Just the screenplay.

Here are three more short paragraphs laden with overwriting and lack of clarity:

EXT. PASTURE - DAY

Antonio (18), Manuel (17), and Gabriel (16), three
handsome, strapping brothers in cowboy wear, are
rising. In the pasture their good-sized flock of
sheep graze peacefully. The youngest sibling,
Gabriel, has just cooked breakfast and served it on
tins to his brothers. Eggs, chile, tortillas,
goat's milk and coffee. They sit around the
campfire on woodstumps and converse casually. Their
sheep-dog, Pancho, vigilantly parked on a hill
over-looking the flock, is a short-haired
Catahoula. Because of their one white eye and
black-spotted coats, they are called jaguar dogs.

Later in that screenplay:

EXT. MORELOS, MEX. - DUSK

On the outskirts of Morelos they pen the sheep and
the horses at the auction stall for tomorrow's
sale. Thousands of cattle, sheep and horses are in
huge wire-fenced lots for tomorrow's sale. Vaqueros
and cowboys from all sides of life crowd the cafe
and cantina. The brothers get their lot numbers
from the bidding agent, and carrying their saddles,

jump a truck into Morelos and get a hotel room, eat, drink, and sleep. Pancho accompanies them.

And still later (after a train ride takes them to Mexico City):

Thousands kneel in the great National Cathedral humming prayers in scores of side-altars and main-aisle pews. The three brothers disembark—Antonio for the leather shops to shop for boots and cowboy hat, Manuel to a cantina to drink and dance, Gabriel to the National Cathedral to pray.

These three paragraphs, broken down into a real shooting script, would take about thirty pages. If anything, they would have to be montages (and we're only on page eight of that screenplay), each of which is a major sequence. This is pure novel writing, prose that defies being a scene in a movie.

Here, on the other hand, is a major car chase with a lot of action, some dialogue, and the whole thing written up in about the time it takes on screen (considerable):

EXT. FAIRMONT HOTEL - SIDE EXIT - DAY

MASON exits the hotel. 20 feet away is the PARKING VALET. 10 incredibly fast expensive European cars are waiting to be parked. First in line, however, is a HUMVEE.

EXT. FAIRMONT HOTEL - SIDE EXIT - DAY

GOODSPEED exits, looking at MASON getting into the HUMVEE. The Humvee explodes out of the hotel driveway.

GOODSPEED shouts to the F.B.I. AGENTS across the street:

                    GOODSPEED
          That's him!

The F.B.I. SEDANS ROAR off after Mason.

GOODSPEED looks around. A Ferrari sitting there.

GOODSPEED gets behind the wheel.

THE FERRARI blasts out of the driveway after the Humvee.

EXT. SAN FRANCISCO - STREETS - DAY

The HUMVEE lumbers up to a traffic light. Stops behind several vehicles ahead.

INT. MASON'S CAR - DRIVING - DAY

MASON looks-up in the rear view mirror. The F.B.I. SEDANS are behind him, closing fast. Mason rams the stick shift into gear; throws the wheel.

EXT. SAN FRANCISCO STREET - DAY

MASON'S HUMVEE veers to the side and CLIMBS OVER a parked, day-glow painted VW BEETLE, squashing it's hood. The Humvee ROARS through the intersection, leaving —

The F.B.I. SEDANS and GOODSPEED'S FERRARI trapped at the light behind the other cars.

EXT. THE STREET AHEAD - DAY

MASON'S HUMVEE plows through traffic, hitting the left and right bumpers of the cars in front of it, knocking them aside. It blows through ten cars like ten-pins.

GOODSPEED'S FERRARI slaloms through the Humvee's wake of dented cars and accelerates after the Humvee.

TWO POLICE PATROLMEN scramble into their cruisers, throwing on the CHERRY TOP LIGHTS.

The CRUISERS charge after the Humvee and the Ferrari.

EXT. SAN FRANCISCO STREETS (HILL #1) - DAY

THE HUMVEE is accelerating up a very steep hill.
100 yards down the hill, the TWO S.F. POLICE
CRUISERS, the F.B.I. sedans, and GOODSPEED'S
FERRARI, all race after it.

INT. MASON'S HUMVEE - DAY

MASON has the radio on. A NEWSFLASH is broadcast:

                    RADIO NEWSMAN
          This just in: More than
          twenty highway patrolmen are
          involved in a high speed
          chase on Van Ness Boulevard,
          north of Trocadero...

MASON looks at Humvee's CELLULAR PHONE. Grabs it.
Studies it. He's never used one before.

                    MASON
          Modern conveniences. Cheers.
          (punches numbers) San
          Francisco. Jade Angelou.
          That's A..n..g..e..l...

EXT. SAN FRANCISCO STREETS (HILL #1)

BUSY DAY AT THE INTERSECTION - THE TRAFFIC LIGHT is
red. A SPARKLETTS WATER TRUCK proceeds into the
intersection.

INT. MASON'S CAR - DRIVING - DAY

MASON runs the red light. The Sparkletts truck is
in the intersection. MASON violently throws the
wheel. The Humvee swerves to avoid the Sparkletts
truck —

EXT. SAN FRANCISCO STREETS (TOP OF HILL #1) - DAY

— but doesn't make it. Mason's Humvee SLAMS into
the Sparkletts truck's BACK END, knocking it

sideways. The HUMVEE blasts through the
intersection as —

70 WATER BOTTLES (5 gallon each) tumble off the
Sparkletts truck. The bottles roll down the hill,
gaining speed.

INT. MASON'S HUMVEE - DAY

The call connects.

>   JADE ANGELOU (O.S.)
>   Hello?

>   MASON
>   Is this Jade Angelou?

>   JADE ANGELOU (O.S.)
>   Yes. Who is this?

>   MASON
>   John Mason. (lengthy pause)
>   Don't be shocked. I don't
>   have much time. Please
>   listen carefully...

INT. GOODSPEED'S FERRARI - DAY

>   GOODSPEED
>   Where is he sir? RIGHT IN
>   FRONT OF ME. What's he
>   doing? HE'S ON THE PHONE. I
>   DON'T FUCKING KNOW, HIS
>   STOCKBROKER! Oh shit. Gotta
>   go.

GOODSPEED looks at SPARKLETTS BOTTLES bearing down
on him.

INT. S.F. POLICE CRUISER - DAY

Two S.F. PATROLMEN. Their eyes widen too as—THE
SPARKLETTS BOTTLES are bouncing now, roll down on
them at 45 m.p.h. A BOTTLE SMASHES through the
windshield, showering the Patrolmen with glass.

EXT. SAN FRANCISCO STREETS - (MIDWAY UP HILL #1) -
DAY

Chaos. Bottle after bottle smashes down on the
front-running vehicles. DENTING HOODS. SMASHING
WINDSHIELDS. THREE F.B.I. SEDANS and GOODSPEED'S
FERRARI negotiate the crashing cars.

They race through the carnage after Mason.

EXT. SAN FRANCISCO STREETS (HILL #2) - DAY

MASON'S HUMVEE explodes over the crest of a hill at
90 m.p.h. and soars. A beat, then —

THE F.B.I. SEDANS, followed by GOODSPEED'S FERRARI
soar over the crest of the hill.

EXT. SAN FRANCISCO STREETS - (BOTTOM OF HILL #2) -
DAY

At the intersection here, TWO S.F. ROAD WORKERS are
sliding a STEEL PLATE over a 6 ft. deep ditch cut
in the asphalt (for a water main or equivalent).

The Road Workers, hearing the WAIL OF MASON'S
HUMVEE, look up and dive away just as THE HUMVEE
blasts over the steel plate, dislodging it from its
positioning. It TEETERS on the lip of the ditch.

THE F.B.I. SEDAN hits the teetering steel plate,
which collapses—causing the sedan to be swallowed
up halfway into the ditch, it's rear end sticking
up in the air. Seconds pass, then —

THE SECOND F.B.I. SEDAN SLAMS into the front
running SEDAN'S EXPOSED UNDERCARRIAGE. Both
vehicles are obliterated.

GOODSPEED'S FERRARI, in the most hair-raising slide
ever filmed, veers and misses the mangled F.B.I.
sedans.

Now it's just MASON and GOODSPEED and

CUT TO:

EXT. SAN FRANCISCO STREETS - (TOP OF HILL #3) - DAY

MASON'S HUMVEE, with GOODSPEED'S FERRARI close behind, races down a street on the crest of a hill.

IN THE INTERSECTION AHEAD - A CABLE CAR is turning down the hill. Mason's Humvee also turns down the hill, but as the Humvee rounds the corner —

AN OLD WOMAN starts crossing the street. MASON throws the wheel swerving to avoid her, and —

— THE HUMVEE'S BUMPER catches the BACK OF THE CABLE CAR, dislodging its rear steel wheels from the CABLE CAR TRACKS. With the front wheels still lodged in the tracks, the cable car begins to slide sideways.

GOODSPEED'S FERRARI clears the cable car's sliding back end and sprints after Mason's Humvee.

EXT. SAN FRANCISCO STREETS - MIDWAY DOWN HILL #3 - DAY

The Humvee and Ferrari blast down the hill. The street is thick with vehicular traffic.

So THE HUMVEE swerves, leaving the street.

onto the sidewalk. Where...SNAP SNAP SNAP it knocks down every parking meter, then hits A LADDER in a cordoned off area. On the ladder, a LINEMAN is fixing a MUNICIPAL POWER LINE. The ladder collapses; THE LINEMAN falls, flailing through the air.

GOODSPEED slams on the brakes. The Ferrari spins 180 degrees and lurches to a stop facing uphill.

INT. GOODSPEED'S FERRARI - DAY

THE AIR BAG'S exploded in Goodspeed's face.

> GOODSPEED
> Shit shit SHIT SHIT...

EXT. SAN FRANCISCO STREETS - MIDWAY DOWN HILL #3 -
DAY

GOODSPEED looks up the hill. GOODSPEED'S EYES bug.

GOODSPEED'S POV - THE CABLE CAR is still sliding
down the hill sideways.

THE SLIDING CABLE CAR, its wheels SPEWING SPARKS
down the hill. The LAST PASSENGER dives. It's
now empty and sliding straight for Goodspeed's
Ferrari...

INT. GOODSPEED'S FERRARI - DAY

GOODSPEED grabs the Ferrari CELLULAR PHONE and
tries the door latch. The goddamn airbag is all
over him...So GOODSPEED shoots the fucking air bag.

EXT. SAN FRANCISCO STREETS - (BOTTOM OF HILL 3) -
DAY

THE TUMBLING CABLE CAR hits the Toyota's rear. The
Toyota gas tank EXPLODES, lifting the cable car.

The Ferrari door flies open. GOODSPEED dives away
as —

— THE CABLE CAR, aflame, cartwheels in mid-air and
lands with a WHUMP on the FERRARI, crushing it like
a tin-can.

GOODSPEED, dazed, wheels away from the wreck,
shielding his eyes from the smoke and fire.

A YOUNG KID ON A MOTORCYCLE rolls up.

```
                  MOTORCYCLE KID
          You just fucked up your
          Ferrari, man.

                  GOODSPEED
          It's not mine.

                  MOTORCYCLE KID
          Way cool. (smiles) 42
```

That gives us the action, the dialogue, and just enough descriptive information ("Top of Hill 3") to keep us properly oriented. It's a clear, visual blueprint for a film sequence.

And now. . .

A WORD ABOUT NOUNS. . .

Brand name writing is very popular in both novels and screenwriting today. Pioneered by novelist Ian Fleming, who gave James Bond Hennessy's Three Star Brandy to drink, handmade cigarettes by Morlands of Grosvenor Street (Balkan and Turkish tobacco) to smoke, and a Beretta .25 to shoot, it's the simple art of saying "a Walther PPK" where Dashiell Hammet would have said "a gun." Or instead of just "a submarine," you write "an Ohio Class SSBN ballistic missile submarine."

. . .AND PURPLE PROSE

A related category is writing known as "hard-boiled" at its best, and "purple prose" at its worst. The line in between is often difficult to navigate. It was done brilliantly by Dashiell Hammett and Raymond Chandler, two writers who turned pulp fiction into high art and created a whole literary genre that has had an enormous effect on films. (If you haven't read their novels *and* seen the films made from them, stop reading and do so at once). It has been imitated by writers ever since, and is very popular in contemporary action screenplays.

Compare:

```
The machine gun opened fire.
```

to:

```
The Uzi spit bullets.
```

There we've added both name brand writing and purple prose. On the other hand, consider:

```
The windshield wipers are beating a slow, erotic
rhythm.
```

Windshield wipers do not react to what is happening inside a car. They have one, two, or three speeds, depending on how fancy the car is, but I doubt any of those speeds are labeled "erotic" in the manual.

Here are a few lines from another screenplay's opening sequence.

```
    The exec tensely watches the vector-graphic
readout from the side-scan sonar array.
    One tail stabilizer is sheared off and the big
screw prangs the wall with an earsplitting K-K-
KWANG!!
    Two foot thick columns of water, like fire-hoses
of the Gods, blast into the room. ⁴³
```

That includes brand name writing (vector-graphic readouts), onomatopoeia (KWANG), and purple prose (fire-hoses of the Gods). But I'm quoting from a very well-written screenplay. It all works here, because this is a high-tech, sci-fi movie that is meant to thunder at you right off the page.

The onomatopoeia (KWANG) works because it's sporadic, and not over-used. The hard-boiled prose is also sparingly done, well written, and balanced with cold, hard, specific action. But most of all, it all works because it's consistent and moves the story forward.

The opening sentence of a screenplay:

```
EXT. STREET - DAY
```

```
The sun beat down on motor city and the asphalt
sweated it back.
```

When I read that, I thought, oh no, one of those tough-guy styles. It's wildly common in screenplays today and usually strained and annoying. But film executives tend to get positively euphoric over things like that, because (for lack of a proper literary education) they think this is the real stuff.

So I can't tell you what to do here, because the same words you write well with might be used badly by the next writer. Name brand writing and purple prose is faddish and, in the opinion of most serious literary critics today, a cop-out, because writing a beautiful, lyric passage on the texture and quality of farm-grown wheat and oats is a good deal harder—so in the end more effective—than saying Kellogg's Frosted Flakes. On the other hand, Kellogg's Frosted Flakes is good shorthand, and the kind of quick phrase best suited to screenplays. Find a style you're comfortable with that gets a positive response from honest critics of your work, and find a style that matches your story.

If you follow the don'ts I have laid out, you are more than halfway toward making your screenplay a pleasurable and impressive read. Now all you need to do is. . .

...WRITE A GREAT STORY.

Part 2

CONTENT

WRITE A GREAT STORY

There probably aren't a thousand stories in the naked city. According to Aristophanes, there are only four. (Simple fortunate, simple unfortunate, complex fortunate, complex unfortunate.) According to Goethe, seven. Georges Polti, writing in 1916, outlined *The Thirty-Six Dramatic Situations*. According to Norman Friedman's *Form and Meaning in Fiction*, there are three plots—plots of fortune, of character, and of thought; each with two possible endings, up or down (making six); and two possible protagonists, sympathetic or unsympathetic (for a total of twelve), then, within plots of fortune, he enumerates categories of action, pathetic, tragic, punitive, sentimental, and admiration. Within plots of character there is maturing, reform, testing, and degeneration, and plots of thought include education, revelation, affective, and disillusionment. (Don't worry, I've lost track too.) Some pessimists think that there are only two stories: Man's Inhumanity to Man, and Man's Inhumanity to Himself. (Dark vision, that.) Shakespeare worked in four styles—comedy, tragedy, historical, and pastoral—so he was a laggard compared to contemporary movie executives, who have a list of genre categories neatly typed for them and always nearby: western, sci-fi (supernatural, horror, fantasy), mystery (hard-boiled/noir/American or literary/intellectual/English), thriller (crime—true or fiction, mob or individual—erotic, psychological, and techno), comedy (romantic, mistaken identity, fish-out-of-water), drama (war, courtroom, historical, family, character, documentary, human, period); action adventure, revenge, disaster, musical, and "women's pictures."

Just as studio executives are constantly trying to figure which categories are in and which are out with an audience, screenwriters are constantly trying to fathom which categories are in and which are out with studio executives. That's a game akin to Rubik's Cube. Just when you think you've got it, it slips away.

Let's trace a few classic stories: *Love Story, West Side Story, Goodbye, Columbus* and *Titanic* are all *Romeo and Juliet. Jaws* and *Anaconda* are *Moby Dick. Pretty Woman* is *Cinderella*, as are *Flashdance* and *Working Girl. Pygmalion and Galatea* became *My Fair Lady* and *A Star is Born; Trading Places* is *The Prince and the Pauper; Edward Scissorhands* is *The Hunchback Of Notre Dame*, which is *Beauty and the Beast*, from which *King Kong* and *Harry and the Hendersons* also derive. *The Nutty Professor* and *Doctor Detroit* are both *Dr. Jekyll and Mr. Hyde*. *As Good As It Gets* is *The Misanthrope*. *Cyrano de Bergerac* became Steve Martin's charming *Roxanne* via a near-exact contemporary adaptation, and *The Truth About Cats and Dogs* is the same story with the sexes reversed. Any number of horror pictures, including all the *Aliens*, are based on Agatha Christie's classic *Ten Little Indians*, a.k.a. *And Then There Were None*. (Or at least, Sigourney Weaver.) You can play this game for hours. I suggest you do. Always steal from the best.

So if there are a finite number of stories, *there is an infinite number of ways to tell them.* (After all, there are only twelve notes in western music, and look how many great songs have been written.) It's all in the writing. Just ask Shakespeare, who took a lot of other people's stories and made them his own.

Good stories tend to be "universal." That is, they touch something deep down in our psyche, what Jung called our collective unconscious. That common id probably goes back as long as the history of thinking Homo Sapiens, which is why folklorists like Joseph Campbell can trace modern stories back to the myths and folk tales of ancient civilizations (known to contemporary audiences as Disney animated films).

If it's not what you write about, but how you write about it, then maybe we should rephrase the rule:

Write a Story Great.

Let's begin at the beginning.

Openings

Alfred Hitchcock said that the difference between an American film and a European film is that a European film can open with a shot of clouds, cut to another shot of clouds, and then cut to a third shot of clouds. If an American film opens with a shot of clouds, it must cut to an airplane, and if by the third shot the airplane hasn't exploded, the audience is bored.

If you are trying to break into the American film market, watch out for too many clouds. Many screenplays do not start quickly enough.

Here is a good rule of thumb: Locate in the script the page where the reader can first identify *what your movie is about*. What is it that the audience is expected to follow curiously. Because until we know that, we're still sitting there, eager, open, and waiting. But your audience will not maintain that state for very long. It is very rare for more than ten pages to go by without the reader having a firm idea of what the film is about. Say ten pages is ten minutes. Twenty pages is twenty minutes. By twenty-five to thirty pages you are almost one-quarter of the way into the picture. If it hasn't started, it's too late.

• *Dirty Harry*—the opening sequence introduces Harry, the second is a murder, and the third is a ransom note, and our whole plot is ready to go in ten pages.
• *Three Days of the Condor*—By page twenty the bookish hero has discovered that all his co-workers have been murdered, and he's out in the cold.
• *Jaws*—the first sequence is the first shark attack. On page twenty-nine the conflict is introduced (the local policeman wants to place warnings, the Chamber of Commerce wants to keep it a secret) and we're off and swimming.
• *Robocop*—The first sequences introduce the nightmare that Detroit has become in the future, and the fact that the police department has been privatized. We meet a policeman, he's nearly killed, he's rushed to a hospital where a little of his original biology and a lot of high-tech gadgetry are combined, and by page twenty-six, the eponymous hero has been created.

Check a few of your favorite movies, and figure when they really get underway.

You know what your film is about, and you've told the reader by a reasonable page. What page is reasonable? That depends on your ability to *hold our interest until we get there*.

There is another way to begin a film. It's a self-contained sequence with a beginning, middle and end. Hollywood studio executives call it The Grabber.

EXT. DEEP SPACE

We OPEN on TOTAL BLACKNESS, a sea of stars spread across the infinite depths of space. As the TITLES ROLL, we notice that three of these specks seem to be moving; one of them picking up acceleration and racing toward us. Our perspective changes, and we catch a quick glimpse as it HURTLES past, and into the gravitational pull of a large brownish planet. Kicking up SPARKS of FRICTION as it hits atmosphere. It seems to be manmade. Or at least artificial.

EXT. PLANET SURFACE - DAY

The planet is dead, barren. Death Valley on a grand scale. We watch the object plummet through the wispy cloud-cover, emitting a few last burning embers before falling to ground way-off in the distance. A BOOMING ECHO resonates across the dusty plains, before settling back into an eerie silence.

EXT. FISSURE CANYON - DAY

We're looking into a deep gorge, dark and sinister. A howling wind whips dust into a sandstorm, reducing visibility to almost zero. About seventy feet down there's a hole in the rock-face that just might be a cave entrance, and near is a peculiar SHIMMERING in the air. We hear a mechanical BEEPING and the SHIMMERING disappears, replaced by FIVE humanoid SHAPES clinging to the sheer rock - each well over seven feet tall. They are PREDATORS, a race of intergalactic big-game hunters on permanent safari; their clothing and weaponry a bizarre mix of aborigine and ultra-hi-tech. In their hands are circular metal discs; 'smart weapons' which cut into the stone and give them purchase.

PREDATOR-VISION. From their P.O.V., we see the fissure reduced to THERMAL HEAT SOURCES. The entrance registers as a black gaping void.

INT. FISSURE NEST TUNNEL

The five hunters climb inside the rim of the
tunnel, out of the wind's banshee wailing. The lead
PREDATOR reaches up to his headgear, pulling at the
coupling pipes connecting it to a hidden breathing-
apparatus. He removes the helmet, clips it to his
rear utility pack, and takes a deep breath of the
air. A curious speckled pattern runs across his
wide forehead, marking him different to the others;
in addition, one of the fangs of his mandibles has
been sheared away. We'll call him BROKEN TUSK, he's
the leader of the hunting party. He reaches out a
hand to caress the wall of the tunnel. Several feet
in from the rim, it changes from rock to a textured
biomechanical surface; a swirling mass of
disturbing shapes. He hurries forward in response
to the GURGLING-HISS of one of his team who has
found something.

The other PREDATOR holds a telescopic spear up for
scrutiny. Skewered on the end is a shriveled FORM
with eight spindly legs and a segmented tail; it's
a FACEHUGGER, the first stage of the deadly ALIEN
lifeform. BROKEN TUSK HISSES a caution to his
party; they respond by pulling spears and
elaborately-shaped swords. Several shoulder-mounted
plasma cannons slide up to firing position,
tracking with their owners' helmets. Thus armed,
they move cautiously ahead...taking no chances. One
helmeted PREDATOR pauses, scanning the area.

PREDATOR-VISION. He switches through a variety of
different views; infra-red, ultra-violet, enhanced
motion-tracking. Nothing.

He's so pre-occupied with this task, he totally
fails to notice the skeletal ALIEN loom up behind
him, emerging from the biomechanical growth on the
floor. A barbed tail skewers the PREDATOR straight
through the neck, splashing luminous blood across
his chestplate. A gargled DEATH-RATTLE issues from
his throat, the band of PREDATORS spinning around
in time to see him being dragged below the ground.

The band of extraterrestrial hunters have no time
to come to his aid; they themselves are set upon by
a half-dozen ALIEN WARRIORS. The carnage is swift
and terrifying, a blur of motion. Steel blades and
serrated biomechanical limbs scythe the air, alive
with the CRIES and HISSES of both adversaries. One
PREDATOR is pinned against the tunnel wall, his
spear out of range. The ALIEN claws away his face
mask, and he finds himself dodging the ALIEN's
toothed tongue, extended toward him with pile-
driver speed. He reaches down, grasping the 'smart-
weapon' hanging from his belt and brings it up in
an arc that terminates at the ALIEN's grinning
face. Big mistake. The two are in such close
proximity that the ALIEN's acidic blood sprays
across the PREDATOR's head. While their technology
seems to be resistant to it, their bodies aren't:
the viscous yellow liquid begins burning into the
PREDATOR's skin. He kicks the skeletal corpse away
with a HIDEOUS PIERCING SCREAM, clawing at his
seared face.

It all seems to be over as quickly as it began;
there can be no question as to who were the
victors. The PREDATORS stand amidst a sea of
biomechanical limbs strewn around like a charnel
house. As his companions begin to carefully
decapitate the ALIEN skulls, BROKEN TUSK steps over
the corpses to examine his fallen comrades. The
first PREDATOR to be attacked was killed instantly;
he crosses to the other. What he finds causes him
to react with pity and disgust. His fallen comrade
is only just alive; mandibles clicking fraily,
half his head burnt away. BROKEN TUSK watches the
ailing PREDATOR slide a steel blade from it's
sheath and offer it to him. He takes it, knowing
what has to be done. Rolling the knife quickly over
the back of his hand - the sort of elaborate trick
seasoned Green Berets perform - he plunges it
downward into the fallen hunter. This unpleasant
task accomplished, BROKEN TUSK straightens up and
activates his wrist-computer. A dark shape blots
out the light coming from the entrance; a small
PREDATOR shuttlecraft, sleek and elegant. It hovers

in the air with little more than a loud HUM, and
extends a ramp. The surviving PREDATORS leap
aboard, carrying their trophies with the reserved
silence of men returning from combat.[1]

Three pages, and if you aren't going to stay for this movie, you
aren't a sci-fi fan.

Exposition

Ex·po·si·tion (ek'spe-zish'an) n. 1. A setting forth of meaning or
intent. 2. The part of a play that introduces the theme and chief
characters.

—American Heritage Dictionary

For the opening scene of *Total Recall*, the ordinary morning of a
working man gives us some ground rules. Quail would like to go to
Mars on vacation, but his wife responds that they can't afford it on
his "lousy ten thousand a week." While eating breakfast, the newspaper is projected on their wall, with the headline "RIOTING ON
MARS OVER WATER TAX." But his wife reads a different ar-
ticle: "Four Women Rape Man in Park," and says "What do they
expect. . .the way men dress these days. . .then they scream rape."
Later, at the

```
INT. SUBWAY STATION - EARLY MORNING

Quail enters the station. Everybody must pass
through a weapons check before proceeding to the
platforms.

TWO ARMED GUARDS stand at either side, as commuters
pass through an electronic beam. On a screen, the
entire body of each person is seen in X-ray. All of
them are clearly carrying a gun in their inside
coat pocket.

                    GUARD
          No weapon again, Mr. Quail?

                    QUAIL
          I keep forgetting, Herb.
          They frighten me.
```

```
      GUARD
Yeah? Well, it's the law,
Mr. Quail. Has been since
1990 they tell me. Tomorrow
- ya carry ya gun or ya get
reported.

      QUAIL
Okay. Herb, okay.²
```

And within four pages, we have several good cultural jokes and a feeling that we're not in the twentieth century any longer, Toto.

Studios like exposition, because it is there on the page, making it easier for executives to understand the characters.

—John Gregory Dunne

What should your exposition consist of?

• It should delineate the chief character's traits that are key to his motivation, the traits that will drive him (willingly or not) to attempt his quest, and the traits he will rely on to succeed. But not traits that we will ooh and aah over, then never see again, because they will appear to be inconsistent with his later behavior. A character's behavior should be consistent throughout your picture. Traits that turn up here and there but do not reappear, and are not subsequently connected to further behavior or plot action, are distracting time wasters.

• It should set out your theme, but **don't give it away entirely.** If you spell out your entire theme early in the picture, the audience has nothing to learn. It's best when we can come to our own conclusions (i.e., yours) as to how life should be lived, gradually, as the hero does.

• Exposition is linked to believability and payoff, two other important items. When a character who we have never seen ride a horse, and have no reason to believe excels in horsemanship, suddenly, in the climax, demonstrates an extraordinary ability at riding and uses it to triumph over his final obstacle, it isn't going to ring true. "Where did he learn to ride like that?" the audience will say, "that's not *believable.*" If that's your story, your exposition needs a scene demonstrating that the hero can ride like Roy Rogers, or your climax will draw guffaws.

On the other hand, when, during your exposition, a character demonstrates an extraordinary ability to ride a horse, and then never rides a horse again during the plot, there is no *payoff*. Although audiences seldom look back and say, "What the heck was that scene for?," the sequence was useless, and you've left something unresolved.

• Really good writing is often distinguished by just how well the exposition is disguised. **Don't spell it out.** Try to hide necessary information within a neutral scene, because (1) "bald" exposition is a classic problem, and (2) if it stands out, then you're telegraphing its payoff. If a character in the first reel casually mentions or demonstrates some skill or knowledge, *apropos of nothing*, it's a dead giveaway he's going to use that in the climax.

• Finally, it should set up the picture's intended style—a.k.a: don't open with a joke if you're going for tragedy. (It's all right to have comedy relief within a tragedy, but your opening sequence should tell us what kind of a picture we are going to read.)

There is a system of directing which writers might bear in mind that states there are five principal dramatic values: style, language, manners, plot and character. Although all are important, the dramatic arts nearly always emphasize one of them over the others. Greek comedy emphasized style (political satire). Greek tragedy emphasized character (think *Oedipus*). The Romans emphasized spectacle (style). Language was paramount for some time (Shakespeare and the Elizabethans), but method acting got so popular in America (character) that it sometimes seemed actors preferred improvisation to text. Woody Allen's humor almost always derives from character, while Noel Coward's derives from manners. Although *Jaws* and other suspense-filled thrillers are plot-driven (make sure you've seen Alan Pakula's riveting *The Parallax View*), the modern Hollywood action film is not. For everything from *Batman* to *Men in Black*, think style. Studios love "high-concept" films, and "high-concept" films are not character or plot driven. Thus special effects have come to play an increasingly important part in film making. Style supports high-concept, and nothing yells style like special effects.

The reason this is a directing concept is that a director must identify his principal dramatic value, and then make all his decisions accordingly. A script often cries out to have a concept. There isn't always a correct answer. I've seen some wonderful productions of Shakespeare directed many different ways. The boring versions are generally boring because they haven't settled on any one specific value. Choosing the wrong value, however, can easily result in failure if the material doesn't support it. On the other hand, choosing the right one (known in Hollywood as a "strong handed" or "visionary" director) can make a good script great.

Story: The successful film *Fatal Attraction* began at Paramount Pictures as a "screenplay based on an original screenplay" by James Dearden (I defy anyone to explain that credit). It was put into production. I happened to read it, and I can tell you that I thought the Gods were crazy. It was boring. A guy cheats on his wife, then can't get out of the relationship? A character-driven picture at a major studio? When I heard the casting, I was dumbfounded. What heterosexual male in his right mind would cheat on Anne Archer for Glenn Close?

The powers-that-be weren't so comfortable either, because at the eleventh hour they paid for a rewrite by Nicholas Meyer, their resident doctor, known to put spin on character. He did. He polished many scenes to a bright sheen, including one in which Michael Douglas and Anne Archer have dinner with their closest friends. (More later on this scene).

The result was a much better script, but in the same style: a character-driven piece, and one in which the characters weren't very sympathetic or interesting. It still lay there on the page like lox. Moreover, it didn't start until page fifty-four, because it wasn't until then that we realized that Glenn Close was a psycho.

I didn't see in the script what director Adrian Lyne saw, because he turned a boring A screenplay into a terrific B movie, by using the story to make a genre horror film. He had chosen Style over Character as his principal dramatic value.

It didn't hurt that marketing managed to make a public issue out of the theme. They got the cover of *Time*; it must have been a slow news week if adultery got the lead. But its success with audiences ($320 million worldwide) is due to the film's strong and consistent horror movie style, a style created entirely by the shooting and editing.

We first see Glenn Close five and one-half minutes into the film, and with her lean and hungry look, electric hair, chain-smoking, and Acting with a capital A, we know at once (because we've been to B movies before) that this woman spells trouble. Species *Vagina Dentata*. At sixteen minutes she has an affair with Michael Douglas (she's insatiable, he feels guilty), and at twenty-five minutes—twice as soon as the script indicated—he says, "You don't give up, do you? You just don't give up?" and we know we have a psycho on our hands. So in the end, the director, if not the writers, started the movie quickly. As for style, every shot, every edit, in *Fatal Attraction* is made with the idea that this is a horror film.

Now, remember the dialogue-rich dinner table scene? Hardly a word of the carefully written conversation is heard by the audience, because the director orchestrated a slow pan over the table while the phone rings louder and louder, then zeroed in on the phone like it was Godzilla pounding on the door. And we know that *the bitch is calling!*

So the last-but-not-least item for your exposition sequence is to make clear your principal dramatic value.

If you've got a good Grabber and subtly woven in your Exposition, you're ready for the rest of the picture. This is a big subject, and probably the principal key to a good read:

Structure

Think of a Hollywood movie as a good roller coaster ride. It has suspense—the long, slow climb to the top without a view of what's coming—twists and turns—sudden changes of direction that surprise you—euphoria—that moment when, in transitioning from one skin-tightening high to a jaw-loosening low, you are, for a moment, in zero G—and climax—your heart just made it through that last loop-de-loop when without warning the bottom drops out. That kind of pacing is what sells Hollywood movies all over the world. And scripts to readers.

Call it a rising line of dramatic action. Or a linear development of related dramatic incidents resulting in a dramatic resolution. Or a sequence of accidents, each following inevitably on the heels of the preceding one. Call it a plot.

In a linear art form (as opposed to painting and sculpture) there is always a start and a finish. You have to begin when the audience is in place, and you have to—eventually—let them go home. How you travel from the former to the later is your structure.

Whether it be defined by Syd Field's three act paradigm:
    beginning - setup
    middle - confrontation
    end - resolution
    with two key plot points, in which the beginning becomes the middle, and the middle becomes the end

or Robert McKee's five part narrative:
    inciting incident
    progressive complications
    crisis
    climax
    resolution

or John Truby's seven major steps:
    problem/need
    desire
    opponent
    plan
    battle
    self-revelation
    new equilibrium

or Linda Seger's eight sections within three acts:
    setup
    development of act one
    first turning point
    act two
    midpoint
    second turning point
    climax
    resolution

or the granddaddy of them all, Joseph Campbell's Monomyth:
>The Call To Adventure
>Refusal of the Call
>Supernatural Aid
>Crossing the 1st Threshold
>Belly of the Whale
>The Road of Trials
>Meeting of the Goddess
>Atonement with the Father
>The Ultimate Boon
>Refusal of the Return
>The Magic Flight
>Rescue from Without
>Crossing of the Return Threshold
>Master of Two Worlds

hardly matters. As far back as Aristotle, writers got much the same advice:

>"A whole is that which has a beginning, a middle, and an end. A beginning is that which does not itself follow anything by causal necessity, but after which something naturally is or comes to be. An end, on the contrary, is that which itself naturally follows some other thing, either by necessity, or as a rule, but has nothing following it. A middle is that which follows something as some other thing follows it. A well-constructed plot, therefore, must neither begin or end at haphazard, but conform to these principles." (*Poetics*)

What does matter, is that you have a structure to your screenplay, however evanescent. Some works of art seem to have barely any structure at all—a Robert Wilson opera, a Philip Glass composition. There once was an off-Broadway "play" in which the cast was a family actually living on the set. They simply went about their daily business, and an audience was ushered in and out nightly (with two matinees). There are wildly entertaining plays in which witty people simply talk to each other for a few hours. *My Dinner With Andre* is often cited as a film in which nothing happens; Andre Serban and Wallace Shawn talk to each other over dinner for one hundred ten minutes. Nevertheless, screenwriting gurus could break down that film into its component parts. Intellectual ideas have as much of a structure to them as does a sequence of actions.

The relevant question for your screenplay will be: what structure does *your* idea need to make it entertaining and effective. In constructing one, remember the dictum laid down by Louis Sullivan, America's first great modern architect:

Form Follows Function

Don't think about three "Acts" when structuring your film. Since dramatists have been talking about beginnings, middles, and endings since time began, we tend to think about drama in three acts, but that's misleading, especially in intermissionless cinema.

More important: are there enough reasons in each sequence— whether it's a one second establishing shot, or a long montage, or a complex, hidden-meaning, dialogue scene between two characters— to warrant the audience wanting to see what happens next? Is there enough *new information* at each turn of the page to keep our interest up? A film may very well have only one actual climax, and it may not come until the very last page. (Or, if it's a network MOW, it may require seven.) What's important is how you maintain the suspense getting there. As Casanova would agree:

Foreplay Before Climax

Put another way by George Abbott, the American theatre's premiere master of timing (and renowned womanizer), "It's better to start slow than end slow."

Don't worry about your page numbers, either: "The first turning point should take place between pages. . ." "The initiating episode must happen before. . ." Instead, make sure that each of your scenes/sequences furthers the story or our understanding of a character. Make sure it gives us something new to digest. *Readers come across scene after scene in which nothing new happens.* Too many stories meander along without focus or dramatic drive.

Worse, some stories change directions half-way through. It's an old proverb, but a sound one: **Don't change horses in mid-stream**. Using any of the popular story structures can help you avoid that, since the answer to your silent queries (Where is my second plot point? What is my inciting incident? Does my resolution address my original question?) can help you focus your story.

The most useful tool for this is the outline, which allows you a clear look at your structure. The tried and true method is the bulletin board, with index cards for each scene. There are screenwriting programs that do the same thing, if high-tech is your preference. Another good device is one of those software programs used by line producers to draw up a schedule. There's a nice little form for each scene, and you can print it out, cut it up, move scenes around, keep old versions, etc. Plenty of teachers suggest making your outline first. There is nothing like having a good road map in front of you to give you the confidence to face all those blank pages.

Here's a different approach: write your first draft, then outline it. Work over your outline, then write your next draft.

It doesn't really matter if you go through the process in a logical order or not. It's exciting to launch right into the script when you have a good idea. But when you finish your first draft, the best way to study your structure is to reduce it to an outline, and go over that.

Some teachers want you to write backwards. If you don't know your ending, they say, you're not ready. Others, on the other hand, tell you to write forward. Let the events go where they should. Both methods should work, because both lead to the same condition: the plot must "hold together," and resolve in a way that the events dictate it should.

Bottom line: **Don't stick with your first draft**. Outline it, and analyze your outline. Remember: the essence of drama is conflict. The escalation of that conflict promotes your plot. Examine your screenplay and ask yourself if there are significant hurdles for your protagonist's struggle.

Whether a plot point is dramatized, told to the audience in narrative, takes place off screen, or is not in its rightful chronological order, **don't leave it out altogether**. When you outline your story, know what each of the steps are, and the order in which they would progress in real life. A story isn't believable unless each of its events grow naturally out of previous events, and characters aren't believable unless their actions are properly motivated. Although mainstream films do tend to be linear—there would hardly be any point to the climactic battle taking place before the preliminary skirmish—

works of art—call them independent films for the sake of convenience—benefit from originality. Once you have your story nicely laid out, the next step may be your most crucial: ask yourself, *What is the best way to tell this story?*

Here is the kind of decision a writer has to make continually: Let's say your damsel-in-distress turns out to be the villain. At what point in the story does our hero discover her duplicity, and at what point does the audience discover her duplicity?

If we spot her before he does, that's suspense. We know she's a baddy, and we're watching him trust her, while we're thinking, "No, don't give her that loaded gun!"

If he spots her before we do, then there's a nice surprise when he says, "Gotcha!" and we think, "Oh, why didn't I spot that?"

If the hero and the audience spot this twist at the same time ("you mean all the time we were making love, you were the one who shot my best friend!"), it gives his character's discovery a strong emotional impact, because we feel the betrayal simultaneously.

We might call the first choice a thriller—it allows us to exploit suspense—the second a mystery—wherein we ought to be at least one step behind the detective—and the third version a drama—because we're empathizing with the character.

In other words, once you have your story points down, you've got to *put them in the most effective order*.

The plot points that make up your structure **don't have to be in chronological order**. Flashbacks comprise the most common re-structuring, and range from the simple bookending of a film with narrative ("Let me tell you how I came to be in this predicament. . .") to more complex cutting, recent outstanding examples of which are Quentin Tarantino's *Reservoir Dogs*, in which the result of a botched robbery is interrupted with continual intercutting to the various participants and how they got involved in the first place, and his multiplot *Pulp Fiction*, in which four stories are intertwined *and* taken out of order, to the extent that a character killed in his own story reappears later to play his part in another. The order of scenes in *Prick Up Your Ears*, the biographical film of playwright Joe Orton, is as chaotic as was his life. Harold Pinter's 1983 film *Betrayal*, from his play, portrays the events of an affair from the end to the beginning, that is, exactly backwards, with each scene taking place a bit earlier in time than the scene it follows. And every writer should read Kauffman and Hart's 1934 play *Merrily We Roll Along*.

Additionally, you **don't have to portray each plot point.** Some events can be taken for granted—e.g. a triggering event, "inciting incident," exposition, could happen before your story begins. It might remain a mystery until later exposure. If you want a family audience, your hero and heroine in a romance are not going to be able to do the consummating deed on screen, yet it may very well be an important part of the plot that they did, or will.

A common error is the repetition of information. **Once you've told the audience, don't tell the characters.** The information will be redundant to us, no matter how startling it is to the characters. Nothing is worse for a writer than to have to relay information a second time, because the audience has already seen it, but the character who needs to know hasn't. If you find yourself in that position, you can either cut away, and the next time we see the character, we'll assume he knows, or go back to your outline and redraw your event timetable. Here is a sequence in which the audience already knows "Mason's" story, but Mason has to tell "Goodspeed."

           GOODSPEED
What is your beef with the
Bureau, anyway Mason? Tell
me.

           MASON
Let's say our countries had
a little dispute. They both
knowingly shafted me.

           GOODSPEED
How?

           MASON
Familiar with the name
Hoover, Goodspeed? I don't
mean a vacuum cleaner...

GOODSPEED listens intently and

                      CUT TO:

Another scene, elsewhere. Then cut back to. . .

```
INT. ALCATRAZ - GOODSPEED'S CELL - MORNING

GOODSPEED stares blankly into space. INTERCUT
between the two cells again.

                GOODSPEED
        Jesus.
            (thinks)
        Why didn't you just tell
        Hoover and the bureau where
        the microfilm was? Make a
        trade? ³
```

So now Goodspeed knows, and we didn't have to hear it again.

You have an adequate number of interesting plot points leading us through your story. You've chosen which ones are important to dramatize, which can be assumed, happen off-screen, or before we pick up the tale. You've put them in their most effective order (considering what you want them to say). Now, how will the reader get to that emotion-packed ending if he doesn't get involved in the first ninety pages? Answer:

Suspense

It could be in the traditional sense, as in a thriller, where we are on the edge of our chair anxious to know if the protagonist will triumph over the antagonist. If he's the star, we know he'll make it, but we suspend our disbelief while we worry *how* he'll make it, or *if* he'll make it *in time*. Or a mystery, where we want to know whodunit. Or in a drama: what will a certain character's volatility cause him to do? And how will it affect others? A comedy: Will this fool step on *another* banana peel, or make it to the end in one piece?

In any case, **don't leave suspense out**. Don't presume that the characters you created are engaging enough to carry us through one hundred pages. Don't think that because the story is autobiographical, we must all be dying of curiosity. Examine your plot outline in the harshest light, and try to answer the question, are there mysteries—of plot or character—for the reader to fathom?

Don't, however, **write random surprises** into your script. Because *inevitability* is the great hallmark of drama.

Your exposition sets out certain facts. Scene Two *must follow inevitably*. And depending upon what happens in Scene Two, Scene Three will take place. In other words, each action is caused by the previous set of actions. And so on until the (inevitable) ending.

But not predictable.

If each scene follows so obviously, we have a suspense-less screenplay. Yet if each scene follows chaotically, without motivation, we lack the inevitability that drives a good plot.

So you are seeking to surprise the audience with what happens, while at the same time convince them that when it does, *it had to*. Thus, the best-ever definition of good plot structure is:

Inevitable, but Not Predictable

In those four words lie the hardest thing to achieve in a plot, and easily the most important. Put another way (by William Goldman), "The secret to an ending is to give the audience what they want, but not the way they expect it." This gives the audience both the surprise they love, and the sense of satisfaction that things went as they should have.

Once you've got all your ducks in some kind of order, it's time to write the

Ending

The unraveling of the plot must be brought about by the plot itself.
—Aristophanes

Truffaut said the perfect ending was a combination of spectacle and truth. Nice line. Truth, meaning that it is the ending dictated by the action so far, not something cooked up by a market research report.

And spectacle. What I think is relevant here is that if each of your plot points bears a certain power, your last should be the most powerful. Failing this is a common fault, so it bears examining. Simplest example is an action picture. If cars crash in the first action sequence, trucks have to crash in the second, and so on, until your finale is a train wreck or something. Same with disaster pictures. If

160

the biggest thing you've got going is a volcano exploding, save it for the climax. If your hero is overcoming a series of obstacles, the last obstacle has to be the most difficult to overcome. If your hero and heroine are going to make love three times, the second time should be better, and the third time should be a real bell-ringer. Bertolucci's *Last Tango in Paris* comes to mind as an example. . .but I'll give you the pleasure of renting it. Many romance films avoid having to come up with bigger and better sex scenes with the simple expedient of saving consummation of the affair until the end. Or skipping it altogether.

All that is no more than common sense structure. Where it gets difficult is with drama. Not every picture has sex or violence as plot points. (Well, some pictures don't.) Often the structure must escalate not with action, but with character revelations.

You also have to be careful to identify your story. *Romeo and Juliet* isn't a romance, it's a tragedy. The structure isn't built on their love blossoming. If it were, Shakespeare would have to top the balcony scene in the second act. *Romeo and Juliet* is built on the obstacles to that love. (And, because it's a tragedy, I guess you could say they didn't overcome them.) Notice how complications in a good farce—from the Marx Brothers to the Farrelly Brothers—increase, until you think that there is just no way out. But there is.

Then again, sometimes there isn't. *Thelma and Louise*—whose ending is certainly filled with both truth and spectacle—is a very dark picture. After an increasingly serious imbroglio that begins innocently enough, there is just no way out for the two girls. So over the cliff they go. Give it to the writer that she resisted the impulse to write a less true ending. (But don't ever quote *Thelma and Louise*. Executives love to tell you how it would have made twice as much money if it had a happy ending.) Perhaps this is a good time to discuss

The time-honoured bread-sauce of the happy ending.

—Henry James

Nothing sells a screenplay better than HEART. If by the end of the read, the reader is emotionally affected, if you have a story that touches people—or scares them, relieves them, makes them happy, or sad—then you've got a strong, probably commercial, story.

Take *The Full Monty*, probably the most successful "foreign" film in America to date, and certainly the most lucrative. (At a cost of $4 million, it has grossed over $244 million. Compare that to the top grossing movie to date: *Titanic*. That one is approaching a $2 billion gross, but it cost $200 million. Do the math. Which one would you rather have invested in?) Maybe *Monty* had a great opening weekend because it was about male strippers, but it had legs— great word-of-mouth—because it packed an emotional wallop. Not because the men finally got up on-stage and bared all, but because we *felt for them*. *Monty* is a film about male self-identity, and its humiliating loss when unemployed. It devotes a great deal of time to the five characters, their lives and backgrounds, and their motivations for joining this hare-brained scheme. Because it does, we empathize, and when the film's single climax finally arrives, it's a big payoff. When all the men doff their hats for their last hurrah, the theatre audience cheers them on, but the cinema audience cheers for them. That's heart.

This is a tough call. Executives know that a film has a better chance of success if the story ends happily, and the audience walks out of the theatre feeling good. Executives don't like to take risks with "downer" endings, it's safer to have heroes and heroines live happily ever after.

But what makes art successful is that it makes the audience FEEL. Not necessarily *good*, but *feel something*. *Romeo and Juliet* doesn't have a happy ending, yet it's enthralled audiences for 400 years.

(In the Yiddish theatre version of *Romeo and Juliet*, however, the lovers awaken from a "sleeping potion," and are re-united. The feeling in Yiddish theatre was, our audiences suffer enough in real life.)

Not since the days of Yiddish theatre have alterations in endings been so heavy-handed as they are in the modern Hollywood development process.

The ending of *Sliver* has stars Sharon Stone and Alec Baldwin clinch in the executive beloved happily-ever-after of stars. The only trouble is, Baldwin is the villain, the pervert who had been spying on her in the shower and killing her friends. The whole film has been written, acted, and directed that way. Re-shooting a new ending because their preview numbers were low and market research suggested it, couldn't change that. Audiences were unhappy with the implausibility of the resolution, and the picture tanked anyway. A good rule might be: if you're going to have a failure, at least make it an honest one.

The charming little off-Broadway musical *Little Shop of Horrors* captured success with a wonderful ending in which the plant that ate people turned on the audience. Tendrils floated out of the ceiling onto theatregoers, and the cast sang the finale (and metaphorical moral): "Don't Feed the Plants." This ending perfectly suited the dramatic arc of the story, and its theme. The director of the film version remained faithful to that ending until the first preview, when the audience gave the film a very low rating. Panic set in. A second preview confirmed that the audience hated the ending, and the production went back into the studio and shot an ending in which the hero and heroine battle and beat the leafy carnivore, and walk off to their idyllic future, an ending completely at odds with the plot and thematic material to that point. Consequently the film utterly fails to deliver the impact that the stage version does.

In fact, if you polled a modern film audience (culled by handing out free screening tickets in malls to people with nothing better to do than go to free screenings—which is exactly the jury studios use to evaluate their films) following an excellent version of *Romeo and Juliet*, they would probably say they hated that ending too. But they don't mean they hated the film, what they mean is, *I'm sorry that everyone died*. Remember, an ending doesn't have to make you *feel good*. It just has to make you *feel*.

Don't get me wrong. There isn't anything fundamentally bad about a happy ending. Unless it is artificially applied. Which brings us back to the interference of film executives.

There are not nearly as many possible options as executives like to think, and they can't just be tacked on. When the appropriate ending of a film is eluding the studio, the problem is either that there's something wrong with the beginning and middle, and no one wants to admit it, or the honest ending—the one that would be *inevitable* based on the preceding scenes—is considered too downbeat by the studio, which is desperately trying to change it against the dramatic will inherent in the piece.

The best advice on the subject of endings won't be good for your career, but it will be good for your writing. **Don't lie**. Stick with the truth as circumstances dictate it. There is a story here, however, that might help.

When the now-classic American musical *A Chorus Line* was in previews, Cassie didn't get the job. That musical's text is based on true stories, and the creator/director, who had been in precisely the position his alter-ego-character is in, didn't give his former lover the job. She wouldn't fit into the chorus any longer. Just before the show opened, however, the director became convinced that the audience had a good deal of emotion invested in Cassie, and wanted to give the audience hope. With his strong nose for the commercial, and for what audiences want, Michael Bennett changed the ending and gave her the job. And so one of the seventeen stories in *A Chorus Line* says, "You can go home again," instead of the truer but darker, "You can't go home again." It's a small thing, but then, the next time you're in a story meeting and your ending and the studio's ending butt heads, maybe you can find a small thing, and effect a compromise.

As long as it's clearly a

Resolution

To resolve or not to resolve, that is the question. And the answer, by Hollywood logic, is: always, always resolve. In spite of the success of the classic short story "The Lady or the Tiger" by Frank Stockton, unresolved plots don't go down well, not with audiences (come on, how many of you read "The Lady or the Tiger" in high school English, and really hated that the author didn't tell you which?) and never with executives (who probably never read "the Lady or the Tiger," as they were too busy reading Donald Trump's biography). But that's just common sense. The fault that crops up so often isn't an unresolved ending, but various unresolved plot points. **Don't leave anything unresolved**, without an awfully good reason. It not only frustrates the reader, but resolution itself is one of the most satisfying things about art.

If your hero is near-sighted, that could be an aspect of his character. But if you *make a major point about his being near-sighted*, bear in mind *you are setting us up*. Sometime before the screenplay is over, his near-sightedness ought to become an issue. If you go out of the way to demonstrate a cowboy's ability to throw a rope, you need to have him throw the rope to accomplish something before your script ends.

In short, to satisfy audiences, endings must satisfy beginnings. If you want to write commercial stuff, if you want to sell spec screenplays to studios, write a story in which the natural, honest ending is a happy one, and conflict is resolved to everyone's satisfaction. But above all, remember that your story must fit together. The final statement must satisfy the premise, the characters must drive the plot, the plot must be realistic for the characters, the genre must not change mid-screenplay, and above all, **don't use coincidence** to get out of your convoluted plot, because

Believability

is probably the single most important issue in the public acceptance of a movie.

The poet should always aim at either the necessary or the probably. Thus a person of a given character should speak or act in a given way by the rule either of necessity or probability.

—Aristophanes

A movie is a slice of life, whether real, surreal, fantastical, past, present, future, verité, or absurd. You can take that life and bend it to the wildest corners of your imagination, as long as you *go there in a dramatically straight line.*

Now to the contrary: In the excellent film version of Michael Crichton's terrific novel, *The Great Train Robbery*, Sean Connery masterminds a Victorian train robbery that ends in a long and suspenseful scene. While the train is speeding through the countryside, Connery has to climb out the window of his own compartment, walk along the top of the train, climb down the side of the baggage car, and, as a confederate inside unlocks the door, climb in where the gold is kept. He then throws the gold out the door of the train to waiting comrades. And returns to his first class compartment back along the top of the train. This is terrific action stuff.

The third time I saw the film, it occurred to me that the plot had one problem. Connery doesn't have to do it at all. His confederate is already inside the baggage car. He's already stolen the gold. He can pitch it out at the assigned crossroads, and the robbery is done. Connery ought to sit the whole thing out in his red velvet seat.

I couldn't help writing to the author, because I was sure I was overlooking something, and wanted to know what it was. Mr. Crichton, who wrote both the original novel and wrote and directed the film, was kind enough to write back. He said, essentially, "It's only a movie."

Not a single critic mentioned this. I never heard anyone say of this film, oh gosh, that plot is full of holes. The lesson is very clear. There are successful movies with holes in their plot the size of the ozone layer.

*But. . .*this is not a lesson the screenwriter can allow himself to learn, because readers and studio executives will take you to task over such things.

In this case Michael Crichton had written the best selling book first, which took him past all those readers and straight to the deal-making phase. Success allows you to do this.

But readers, or "story analysts," love to pounce on a thing like that because it can, with a careful parsing of the plot, be irrefutable, and because it's easy to do, if you have a reasonable grasp of logic.

But *believability* is not always linked to logic. Executives love to say, "I didn't believe she would. . ." and etc. What they are really saying is *"You didn't make me believe it."* That's an entirely different thing.

So your set-up is everything. If your major character is from the planet Krypton, which has much stronger gravity than Earth, then it stands to reason (within dramatic license), that when he arrives here, he will have super-powers.

In Goldman's *Marathon Man*, nebbishy student Dustin Hoffman is pitted against experienced villains. Doesn't have a chance, you say? But he has one talent, which has been established from page one: he can *go the distance*. He's a marathon runner. (Common plot: ordinary person thrust into extraordinary circumstances rises to the occasion. Key to making it work: the tools he uses are part of his original character.)

How did Jimmy Stewart triumph over so many Evil Institutions? Because he had moral integrity on his side.

Lately we've had two Presidents of the United States single-handedly defeat alien armies and organized terrorists. Preposterous, you say? (You'd be right.) But early in *Independence Day* and *Air Force One* the writers establish that both fictional presidents have war-hero backgrounds. (In fact, John F. Kennedy served on a PT Boat, George Bush was a pilot, and a number of current congressman are Vietnam Vets, so we have a tenuous but adequate link to reality.) It's enough, because it's the *premise*.

Tell us something—anything—up front, and when subsequent actions are based on that fact, we'll buy them.

Because the audience always exercises what is known as their *willing suspension of disbelief.* That's an academic theory for the common practice of believing what they are told. If in the opening scene you establish that boy-from-Iowa meets girl-from-Minnesota, then it is unlikely that the boy can suddenly speak French in the finale. But if you've established that the boy is from France, then he can say something romantic to the girl in French. It may come as a surprise to her, but we'll buy it. In other words, stick to reality— not reality itself, but the reality that you have created. Then your characters and the actions they take will be believable.

A corollary of this is the innocent girl who goes into the house we know is filled with slimeball gargoyles who happen to have a diet of sorority coeds. And you're thinking—you're the audience now—*Are you crazy! Don't open that door!* But of course she does, and of course you expect her to, and of course it's what you want because *you too want to see what's behind the door.* This is a narrow call but let's see if we can't come to some conclusions about right and wrong. I would say that if we can establish this girl as a dimwit, or if she has an overpowering need to look inside—maybe she lost her friend and this is where she thinks she is—then okay. Maybe to her the house is perfectly safe. (We know better.) Okay, that makes sense. But if you're going to write that she has just fought her way out of a first closet containing coed-eaters, then probably her peeking in the next closet is going to look pretty stupid. There are entire films based upon this kind of thing, and they all make money so who am I to say not to write it. I won't. But at least set up a premise in which we can believe that this woman is in need of walking into haunted houses and checking out all the closets.

Theme

It is well-nigh time that people ceased talking about the form of dramatic compositions, about their length and shortness, their unities, their beginning, middle, and end, and all the rest of it; and that we now began to go straightway to their contents, which hitherto, it seems, have been left to take of themselves.

—Goethe

Hollywood lately has set a premium on violent encounters between the hero and the villain. Action sequences have come to be calculated like the musical sequences in Broadway musicals—i.e. you've got to have an "opening number," a "nine o'clock number," a "first act finale," an "eleven o'clock number." Each has to escalate, providing greater and greater thrills over the previous sequence. Thus the violence itself has come to be the entertainment, in films that are little more than entertaining. I'm not going to argue against that. (How could I, in a book about screenwriting?) But I would like to remind you that the strongest scripts are (or, are also) *about something.*

I'm not knocking writing a genre film. In fact, I'm suggesting it. As Willie Sutton said when they asked him why he robbed banks, "Because that's where the money is." Domestic grosses are rapidly being dwarfed by foreign grosses. Studios are targeting worldwide audiences. Worldwide audiences, especially those who don't speak English, like action films with a minimum of dialogue, and physical shtick for comedy. Literary puns don't get guffaws in the Bombay bijou.

But the most important thing in writing is a theme. Something to sing about. Something worth writing about. The reason I loved *Robocop* is that underneath all that action there was a wonderful theme—too much capitalism breeds a new fascism. A dictatorship by private concerns. He who has the most money sets the law. The screenwriters' view of the future of rampant capitalism was clear, and presented in a more entertaining manner than Karl Marx ever did.

We learn best when we are emotionally involved. So **don't lecture.** There always pops up in bad screenplays that one paragraph where the author has put his theme into the mouth of one of his characters. It's usually strained, because people don't talk like that. Let us draw our own conclusions. You just write a story that invokes that conclusion.

Many writers write down their theme and tape it to their keyboard, or to their morning mirror. Many teachers suggest doing this. I do too, if not literally. *Know your theme.* Keep in mind what you are trying to say. Moreover, *have* something to say. We *want* to learn something. That's human nature.

•   •   •

Enough about bad screenplays. Let's talk about good screenplays for a moment. Especially money screenplays. (Not good writing. You're on your own there.) A good screenplay features (among other things) the following three items:

Character, Twists, and Whammies

These are the things that make an executive's heart start racing. If you want to sell a screenplay, the more of each you have, the better.

Taking them one at a time. . .

Character

```
              BERT
     You got talent.

              EDDIE
     I got talent? So what beat
     me?

              BERT
     Character. ⁴
```

It will come as no surprise to even the novice writer that good characters make for good drama. One particularly eloquent teacher aphorized:

Character Is Drama

Hamlet drives *Hamlet*. Richard III *Richard III*. Karl Childers, played by Billy Bob Thornton, makes of *Sling Blade* a mesmerizing movie. Dustin Hoffman, the first short, Jewish, big-nosed, sad sack actor with terrible posture and a shuffling, self-conscious gait ever to become a major movie star, altered the cinematic stereotype of a hero with the sheer power of great comic acting in *The Graduate*. (Paving the way for Richard Dreyfuss, after which Hollywood threw away the mold and went back to hunks.)

The question becomes, how can you bring good characters to a Hollywood movie today, in which any pause from the action to delineate character makes an executive nervous, and if it's not cut in the rewrites, it will be in the editing room.

Answer: plot and character are not mutually exclusive. Because:

Character Is Destiny

How a character goes about his activity—whether it be thinking (Gene Hackman played his saxophone in *The Conversation*), assassination (Edward Fox was methodical to the point of obsession in *The Day of the Jackal*), or running for Congress (reluctantly, as Robert Redford does in *The Candidate*)—can be an opportunity to define his character.

Let's start at the beginning. As with stories, the primary roles have all been well-categorized:

At the dawn of literature:
    The Protagonist
    The Antagonist
    The Chorus

In Comedia Dell'Arte:
    Scapino (the top banana)
    Harlequin (the second banana)
    Pantalone (the ridiculous old man)
    Dottore (the pompous, meddling crony)
    Captain (the inflated ego)
    Scaramouche (the sad fool)
    the Servants - gossipy and clever
    and of course, The Lovers

And by Joseph Campbell:
    The Herald
    The Hero (whom destiny has summoned)
    The Protective Figure
    The Threshold Guardian
    The Goddess/Queen
    The Trickster

- Our Hero.

The hero/good guy/central character/protagonist *performs the decisive action of the story.* **Don't take the picture away from the hero.** Especially in the climactic moments. (Unless the person we thought was the hero, turns out not to be. Good twist.) Usually he has some good qualities, anything ranging from being able to leap tall buildings at a single bound to a quiet stick-to-itiveness, and usually, though certainly not always, the audience identifies with the hero, sees the events from his point of view.

Any functioning character can be male or female, of course. Interestingly, Hero was a female in Greek mythology, a priestess of Aphrodite, beloved of our boy Leander. Although Webster defines "heroine" as a female hero, i.e., the protagonist of a story, most dramaturgs think of the heroine as the damsel-in-distress, the girl for whom the hero slays the dragon, not a female dragonslayer.

"Anti-hero" seems a little weak a phrase for those wonderful leading men—from Richard III and Macbeth to Rodgers and Hart's infamous Pal Joey to the many fascinating killers in Martin Scorsese's Mafia Movies—who aren't very admirable. Rather say, an "unsympathetic hero."

Executives want the audience to sympathize with at least one character, and they tend to lean toward the largest role. The largest role in *Citizen Kane* is Kane, and he's a hard man to sympathize with. He's rich, stubborn, and blind to everyone around him. Still, we've seen the boy Kane. We feel sorry for Kane—the wealthiest man in the world is still unhappy. (Nice to know that, isn't it?) When an executive says, let's root for so and so, it isn't necessarily the same thing as sympathy.

What an audience needs to do is *empathize,* which gives us a little more leeway. Webster defines *sympathy* as a "sameness of feeling," "a mutual liking or understanding," and an "ability to share another's ideas or feelings." Webster defines *empathy* as "intellectual or emotional identification with another." If your character is *understandable,* if his conduct is believable within the average person's sphere of understanding (given your premise), then audiences are likely to identify with him/her. We know we're not perfect, and we can identify with imperfections too.

Audiences tend to like things that reinforce their own prejudices. But artists tend to want to change those prejudices. Brecht said we go to the theatre to find a better way to live. Film investors want to attract large audiences, not give artists a platform. There isn't always a common ground, but empathy with your story and characters is where to look for one.

Not every character has to change. In *Raging Bull* Jake LaMotta crashes through his life making all the same mistakes again and again. His explosive temper, his lack of intelligence, and his profession (boxing) are a bad match. We fade out on the man stubbornly banging his head against the wall of a jail cell. He hasn't learned a thing.

But *we* have.

That's great art, and no matter how many executives tell you that *Raging Bull* didn't make any money, was a depressing film that no one went to see, and that they don't want to make that kind of film, it does not negate the fact that *Raging Bull* is one of America's film masterpieces, on nearly every critic's ten best list of the Twentieth Century.

Call it "the burning building syndrome." Notice how many people stand around watching a fire. How the opposite lane slows down and gawks at an accident. We are often mesmerized by a character's flameout ("Look at me, Ma, on top of the world!"[5]). We can even set aside our morality temporarily in order to sympathize with them. Although the Corleone clan does not rate our sympathy, they get it because *The Godfather* doesn't portray them as crooks, but as a loyal, close-knit family fighting a war against other, less moral, crime families and corrupt cops. From that point of view, their multi-generational saga is as fascinating and empathetic as Horatio Alger.

In other words, whether you have written a genuine hero or an anti-hero, he must remain the focal point of your story. He (or she) must address the challenges of his journey, successfully (comedy and drama) or unsuccessfully (tragedy).

If the plot structure is the hero's physical journey, the character arc is his emotional journey. It is useful—though not always necessary—for a hero to be effected by events which in the end alter his character.

Redemption ("The act of fulfilling a pledge, to set free, salvation from sin") is a common character arc among heroes. For *Cliffhanger*, Sylvester Stallone—always a strong protector of his popular character—insisted on adding the opening scene, in which his high mountain ranger rescue fails and a girl falls to her death.

This destroyed his confidence, which he was then able to recover (redeem) through his heroic actions in the subsequent story.

Another is the learning curve, or growth. A misanthrope can learn to like people (Dickens' Scrooge, the neighbor in *Home Alone*), an unrepentant chauvinist may come to appreciate women as equals (Michael Douglas in *Romancing the Stone*), a group of men may regain their self-confidence (*The Full Monty*).

Regarding ensemble pictures: you simply have more than one hero. Or, better yet, your hero is divided into multiple parts, the majority of the characters addressing the same challenges. (*M*A*S*H* = Hawkeye and Pierce; *The Dirty Dozen* = the whole platoon.)

On the other hand, the fact that one-man plays are popular (especially with actors) tells us you don't need to have all the character categories physically represented. You could argue forcefully, however, that they always are present, even if one man has to play all the parts. (After all, sometimes we are *our own worst enemy*.)

• The Hero's Helpers
    Examples of the mentor/wiseman/ guide/teacher/ friend range from Merlin and Old Ben Kenobi to the tough-but-fair cop/sergeant/teacher/father. His/her position in the screenplay is usually to give some guidance to our hero, who usually evidences some Achilles heel he has to overcome before reaching the end of his quest. Ben Kenobi, of course, teaches Luke Skywalker to use the Force. On the comic side, graduate Benjamin Braddock gets one keyword of advice for his future from a friend of the family: "Plastics." This doesn't quite have the intended effect, instead it stands for everything the graduate is terrified of, but you'll notice it does a good job of defining the graduate's inner conflict for him and for us.
    Sidekicks are my personal favorite. Most often they supply something the hero is missing: common sense (Sancho Panza), modesty (Dr. Watson), skills (Tonto), femininity (Emma Peel), a conscience (Jiminy Cricket), a foil (Ed Norton), a warning (Ethel Mertz), a moderating influence (Colonel Pickering). They're very useful when the hero wants to express some inner thoughts without breaking the fourth wall, or the writer needs to catch the audience up on events without having the hero talk to himself.

• Hiss. . .

Villains/antagonists come in all shapes and sizes, and needn't be unilaterally evil. A great piece of writing is in *Little Giants*. When the coach-of-the-opponents against our struggling little football team chastises a helpful parent for telling a player to deliver a low blow, the parent responds:

```
             DAD
   I thought you wanted to win?
```

And the villain of the piece instantly humanizes himself with

```
             COACH
   Not that way. ⁶
```

•   •   •   .

Early on in theatre the idea of a character featuring a single, overwhelming characteristic became popular. Ben Jonson (as in the subsuming greed of *Volpone*), and Moliere (the hypochondria of *The Imaginary Invalid*), utilized this new dramatic device better than anyone ever had, and since then it has become extremely popular (Shylock, Fagin, Melvin). To the modern action film or slapstick comedy it is invaluable, since there is hardly time to develop a more detailed character. Examples include

. . .the "cynical" cop (his wife left him because of his obsession/hours/drinking),

. . .the "standoffish" woman (just got out of a bad relationship and is wary of a new one),

. . .the "harried" single mother (struggling to raise her one very cute child),

. . .the "eccentric" scientist (have you ever met one who wasn't?),

. . .the "rigid" authority figure (doomed to either be shot in a drama or embarrassed in a comedy), and

. . .the "slovenly" bachelor (if he can't take care of himself, who will?).

Another popular trait is the flouting of authority, whether it be by a rogue cop (Clint Eastwood's Harry Callahan), anarchic citizen (Jerry Lewis, Jim Carrey), an anti-establishment figure (Mel Gibson's Mad Max), or a true misfit (Jack Nicholson in *Easy Rider*, Jack

Nicholson in *One Flew Over the Cuckoo's Nest,* Jack Nicholson in *Five Easy Pieces*).

Obsession is also a good character trait (Richard Dreyfuss in *Close Encounters of the Third Kind*), as is anything that runs counter to traditional character traits (women who are strong, men who are sensitive, children who are evil). So is a hidden agenda. (Why won't the heroine sleep with the hero? Answer in last reel.)

If these are all clichés now, it's only because they've been so useful for so many decades. Movies, after all, are in a kind of dramatic shorthand, and true depth of character—available to writers of prose and plays—is more often supplied to films by the charisma of an actor in close-up.

The writer who comes up with a new one will have Hollywood beating a path to his door.

Perhaps we might hypothesize that in today's movies, one strong character trait is worth half a dozen subtle ones. In any case, if you want to sell a screenplay, take a close look at your lead and make sure that buried in his psyche is something that can motivate him. If you can make it unique, all the better. Sometimes a single character trait can drive a script to above average success. Here is a scene that introduces a unique protagonist:

EXT. BENEATH THE PIER - NIGHT

FOUR TOUGH-LOOKING DOCK WORKERS are camped out under the pier, warming themselves around a small bonfire, laughing loudly. Christmas decorations dangle above them from the pier, and empty beer cans litter the sand around them.

CAMERA PUSHES IN to discover an old collie tied to one of the pilings. Then we realize that the dog is being tormented by the dock workers. They flick lighted matches at him. Shake their beers and spray him in the face. These guys are not rocket scientists.

The dog cowers, tugging on the rope. Tries to get away. All to the great amusement of its tormentors.

One of them turns, laughing—

As a shadowy FIGURE strides calmly up to the fire:
Long hair. Cigarette dangling from lower lip.
Shirt-tails hanging loose below the waist.

Nothing threatening in his manner as he plops down
beside the men, smiling. They are immediately on
their guard.

                    RIGGS (FIGURE)
            Happy holidays. Mind if I
            join you?

                    PUNK #1
            Yes.

                    PUNK #2
            Fuck off.

Riggs smiles at him innocently. Strokes the
collie's fur with one hand. With the other, he
reaches into a paper sack and extracts a spanking
new bottle of Jack Daniels, possibly the finest
drink mankind has yet produced.

                    RIGGS
            I need help drinking this.
            Cool?

The dock workers exchange glances. There seems to
be no harm in this. One of them frowns:

                    PUNK #1
            You a homo?

                    RIGGS
            Do I look like a homo?

                    PUNK #1
            You got long hair. Homos got
            long hair.

                    PUNK #3
            I hate homos. Arrggh.

Riggs shakes his head, laughs.

>   RIGGS
>   Boy, you guys are terrific.
>   You make me laugh, you just
>   do.

At which point, appropriately enough, Punk #4
shakes a beer and sprays it in the old collie's
face.

The DOG pulls away, WHINING. Riggs leans forward.

>   RIGGS
>   This your dog? Nice dog.

And then, he proceeds to do a peculiar thing: He
starts to talk to the dog—in what seems to be the
dog's own language. Very weird, folks...He coos,
snuffles, barks softly, then withdraws, listening,
his ear to the dog's muzzle. Riggs nods. Frowns.
The others look on, puzzled. Then Riggs looks at
each of the four dock workers.

>   RIGGS
>   Huh - You know what? He says
>   he doesn't want you to spray
>   beer in his face. He says he
>   just hates that.

A pause. Uncomfortable. Then—

>   PUNK #1
>   Oh, he does...? (beat) Well,
>   mister, why don't you ask him
>   what he likes...?

The others snicker. Riggs simply nods.

>   RIGGS
>   Okay.

And once again, begins to confer with the dog.
Listens intently, piecing together what he is
hearing.

> RIGGS
> What...? You want...oh. Oh,
> hell no, I couldn't do
> that...Nossirree bob, you
> little nut.

He ruffles the dog's hair. The men are more puzzled
than ever as Riggs turns and says:

> RIGGS
> (chuckling)
> Get this: He wants me to
> beat the shit out of you
> guys.

Everything stops. A cloud passes over the assembled
faces and a pin-dropping silence ensues.

Riggs, completely heedless, once again attends to
the dog:

> RIGGS
> What's that...? The one...in
> the middle...'is a stupid
> fat duck'...What...?
> (listens again) Oh-...Oh! A
> 'stupid fat fuck!' Right.

He looks up, shakes his head.

> RIGGS
> Boy, this dog is pissed.

The one in the middle grabs Riggs by the collar.
Hoists him to his feet. Gulp.

Stands, staring down at Riggs, whose eyes are
completely neutral, like a snake's.

> PUNK #1
> Buddy, you're shortening
> your life span.

He flicks open a mean-looking switchblade.

Riggs is dead meat.

So why then, does he choose this moment to execute
a Three Stooges' routine, consisting of nose tweak,
eye gouge, and rotating fist that bobs the dock
worker on the head...?

He's nuts or something...

Riggs steps back and adopts a neutral fighting
stance. The others begin to circle.

The DOG BARKS. Riggs turns to the dog, but his eyes
never leave his grinning attackers.

> RIGGS
> (to the collie)
> What's that...? You
> want me to take the knife
> away...and break his
> elbow...?

Circling...

Riggs, watching them, his eyes beginning to
dance...Breathing slow and even...

> RIGGS
> But that would be
> excruciatingly painful...

Something inside Riggs is gearing up...the
others can perhaps sense it, their smiles falter
a bit, they crouch, combat-ready...Riggs, eyes
blazing...

> RIGGS
> And if I separated the fat
> one's shoulder...he'd
> probably scream...

No doubt about it. We know from the look in Riggs'
eyes he's nuts. He wants the fight, badly, all four
of them at once...

And then Punk #1 springs...Big mistake.

Needless to say, mincemeat is made of the four
meddlesome dog-torturers.

The beach is littered with their writhing forms as
Riggs does, finally, what he set out to do:

Unties the dog.

Starts to go. As he does, he pats his shirt...

Pats his jeans...Realizes his wallet has flown free
during the fracas.

Scoops to retrieve it from its resting place on the
sand,

where it lies open, and as it lies open, yes,
folks, that is a badge we see.

Riggs, we realize, is an officer of the law.

He lights a cigarette and notices the collie,
seated. Frowns:

>   RIGGS
>   Okay, skeezix. Go on. Get
>   outta here.

He begins to walk away. The dog remains close at
his heels. Following him.

>   RIGGS
>   No, no. Don't follow me. I'm
>   an asshole. Go away.

The dog sits obediently and Riggs walks away. He
can't help it, looks back over his shoulder...

Sees the dog watching him with a beseeching
expression. Pitiful.

```
                    RIGGS
            Aw, shit.

He signals the dog.

                    RIGGS
            Awright. Move it. Let's go.

The COLLIE BARKS happily and dashes toward him
through the surf, kicking up sand and water.

As they shuffle off against the palm-lined skyline,
we hear, supered, Riggs' voice.

                    RIGGS (V.O.)
            So. You live in the area?
            What's your major...?
```

Although also an action scene—see Whammies below—that scene's principal job is to introduce the hero's character. Not your ordinary cop. Later in the same script we meet an entirely different kind of policeman:

```
EXT. MURTAUGH'S HOUSE - PRE-DAWN

Palm trees cast shadows on the lawn. Toys, lots of
them, littered across the lawn. A Big Wheel, a G.I.
Joe figure. Christmas lights are strung across the
eaves.

                                        CUT TO:

INT. HOUSE - BATHROOM - SAME

A real gun, a .38 Police Special, dangling in its
holster from the back of a chair. Next to it—A real
badge, gleaming in the light. It identifies its
owner as LAPD Robbery/Homicide.

ANOTHER ANGLE

A birthday cake comes INTO FRAME. A set of matronly
hands places it directly in front of—
```

DETECTIVE ROGER MURTAUGH

Seated in the bathtub. He groans, throws a towel
over himself, and mutters in mock indignation.
Roger is tough: an old-fashioned fighter, wears his
past like a scar. Piercing eyes; cynical. He is
surrounded by his family; wife and three children,
names and ages as follows: TRISH: Roughly thirty-
eight. She used to be a stunner. NICK: Ten years
old. Precocious. CARRIE: Age seven. Eyes like
saucers. Adorable. RIANNE: Heartbreaker stuff,
Seventeen. Takes your breath away folks. The cake
is a real beauty.

> CARRIE
> Make a wish, Daddy.

> RIANNE
> Go for it, Dad.

> MURTAUGH
> (smiles)
> Go for it, huh...? Okay,
> I'll go for it.

He blows out the candles. Applause. His gaze
lingers on—the cake. Or rather, the message
scrawled atop it in icing:

WELCOME TO THE BIG 50

The presents arrive.

> CUT TO:

INT. MURTAUGH HOME - SAME TIME

And it is a typical morning for Detective Roger
Murtaugh. Chaos. The TELEVISION BLARES. Young
Carrie Murtaugh wails like a banshee. Her brother
Nick tells her to shut up. Trish Murtaugh is
burning eggs in the kitchen. Roger Murtaugh enters
then, fixing his tie. The following dialogue is
fast and furious, tossed over the shoulder as
Murtaugh scurries to and fro, getting dressed:

                    MURTAUGH
          Honey, what's this on my
          tie?

She looks.

                    TRISH
          An ugly spot?

                    MURTAUGH
          Thanks. Sharp as a pin.

                    TRISH
          I'm thinking of going on
          'Jeopardy.'

                    MURTAUGH
          Don't take any questions on
          cooking.

                    TRISH
          Thanks. I love you, too.

Carrie is still shrieking. Tears stream down her
face.

                    MURTAUGH
          Hey, kid, turn off the
          waterworks, okay?

                    CARRIE
              (points to Nick)
          Daddy, he changed the
          channel!

                    MURTAUGH
          NOOOOOO.

                    NICK
          She's a crybaby, Dad.

                    MURTAUGH
          Mind your own business.
              (nods toward the TV)
          That's illegal.

                    NICK
          What's illegal?

                    MURTAUGH
          Can't put a dead body in an
          ambulance. This 'Kojak'?

                    NICK
          'Starsky and Hutch.'

                    MURTAUGH
          Huh. It's illegal. Never put
          a dead body in an ambulance,
          son, you got that?

                    NICK
          Sure, Dad.

                    MURTAUGH
          Honey, where's the spot
          remover? (turns to Carrie)
          Young lady, stop crying or
          I'll give you something to
          cry about. Damn.

He dabs at his tie. Carrie screams. In the kitchen
Trish drops the eggs, swears. The PHONE RINGS.
Carrie screams.

                    MURTAUGH
          That's it. I'm gonna give
          you something to cry about.

He grabs a copy of Newsweek and hands it to her.

                    MURTAUGH
          Starving children. See? They
          haven't eaten, it's very
          sad. Cry.

He moves away.

                    CARRIE
          Daddy, you're weird...

MURTAUGH
Thank you, Carrie. Hear
that, honey, the children
think I'm weird.

TRISH
They're bright children.
(hangs up the telephone)
Honey, you know a man named
Dick Lloyd? Don't step in
the egg.

MURTAUGH
Where's my thinking? I
should've checked the floor
for egg. Dick Lloyd...?
(beat) Jesus, Dick Lloyd.
What's he want?

TRISH
The office called. He's been
trying to reach you for
three days now.

MURTAUGH
I haven't talked to him
in...shit, twelve years? No,
wait a minute, that would
make me fifty years old,
that can't be right.

TRISH
    (smiles)
You're not getting older,
you're getting better.

MURTAUGH
Inform the children of this.
(kisses her; heads for the
door) Forget the eggs, I'll
eat later.

> TRISH
> Whatever. (Beat) Honey? (as
> he stops) How come I never
> heard of Dick Lloyd?

> MURTAUGH
> I never talked about him.

> TRISH
> Oh. (Beat) Vietnam buddy?

> MURTAUGH
> Yeah. Vietnam buddy.

He exits the kitchen, crosses the entrance hall.
Stops, noticing Rickles the cat, who is happily
munching on the remains of Roger's birthday cake.

> MURTAUGH
> Hey.

He swats it aside. Pauses, his gaze lingering on
the silent message which gnaws at his guts.

THE BIG 50...

He comes out the front door. Flicks off the
Christmas lights, crosses to the car. Looks up, and
sees his oldest daughter Rianne. Jogging past. She
wears an adorable pair of dolphin shorts. Walkman
headphones. She waves.

> RIANNE
> 'Bye, Daddy.

He waves.

> MURTAUGH
> (shakes his head)
> Goddamn heartbreaker. She's
> a heartbreaker.

So now we've met two cops, with distinct, and distinctly different, characters. Shortly thereafter, they meet:

ACROSS the room, a detective takes off his gun and slings the holster across his chair. As he EXITS FRAME—PAN to reveal: Martin Riggs as he enters the squad room. Shuffles from foot to foot, looking lost. Lights a smoke.

ACROSS ROOM

Murtaugh slings on a jacket. Turns to go. Notices Riggs.

MURTAUGH'S POV

Riggs resembles a bag person. Unshaven, limp dirty hair, grimy leather jacket.

BACK TO SCENE

He frowns, says:

> MURTAUGH
> McCaskey, if my wife calls,
> tell her late dinner.

> BURKE
> Ho, Rog - I'm not through
> yet. I'm supposed to tell
> you two more things.

> MURTAUGH
> Shoot.

He is still looking at Riggs, who is slowly wandering from desk to desk, smoking — Stopping near the desk with the holstered gun.

> BURKE
> First, condition of the
> sheets and mattress indicate
> someone was in bed with
> Amanda Lloyd just before she
> died. That's A.

> MURTAUGH
> What's B?

                    BURKE
          B is, I'm supposed to tell
          you you're breaking in a new
          partner on this.

Now Murtaugh is eyeballing Riggs. Cautious.

                    MURTAUGH
                (distracted)
          I don't work partners.

                    BURKE
          You do now. C.I.T. transfer,
          some burnout they want you
          to keep on a leash.

                    MURTAUGH
          Oh, perfect. Can I trade in
          my life for a new one?

At which point, across the room, Riggs removes the
holstered gun and hefts it, curiously. Suddenly all
hell breaks loose.

                    MURTAUGH
          Gun!!

He bolts like a cheetah. Cops dive for cover, a
secretary shrieks, and Murtaugh goes plowing
through the squad room like an express train,
blowing people out of the way — Cops grabbing for
their holsters — Riggs, meanwhile, looking around
frantically, he's trying to find the guy with the
gun who is, of course, himself.

Murtaugh takes a flying leap, sails across the
desk, going for the glory. And Riggs, in the blink
of an eye, simply ducks and flips Murtaugh neatly
over one shoulder. There is a hideous crash of
BREAKING GLASS and OVERTURNING FURNITURE.
Ouch...McCaskey, meanwhile, screams to Burke:

                    McCASKEY
          What the shit is going on?

Burke sighs, shakes his head:

> BURKE
> Roger just met his new
> partner. [7]

Not only are both leads introduced to the reader in scenes which clearly define their principal characteristic, but the clash of their characters is well-established, a conflict far more germane to the screenplay's interest (and the film's success) than whatever conflict exists between the good guys and the bad guys. (I defy you to remember the actual story line of *Lethal Weapon*.)

Strong characters like Riggs sell screenplays, because *the studios want roles for stars*. And producers know that stars say yes to clearly defined, fun-to-play roles.

No writer sets out to write a bad role. But what I'm talking about is a little beyond just the quality of the writing. You want a role that a producer can visualize as being played by a star. Stars don't want to do anything unheroic, don't ever want to disappoint their audience (who they talk about with an incredible love/hate relationship) and most of all they are dreamers. They actually see themselves as the roles they play, and they think a lot of themselves, so the roles they play have got to be as close to supermen as you can make them. If your screenplay has a role like that, they might like to play it. What's important to you is that *the studios know that*. You've written a commercial film because it has a role for Arnold, Clint, Sly, Bruce, Mel, or Will. Probably you won't get one of them because they're booked three years in advance, and their agent won't even look at a script unless there is a check attached. What matters is that you've written a strong role and producers/studios will see it that way. By the time they get down the list and start offering it to the B list, the ball is rolling and you've got a chance of getting a film made.

You know that index card you've got on your bulletin board with the name of your hero on it? Make sure there is a strong, interesting character trait under the name, and **don't forget to express it** within the character's actions and dialogue.

One way to approach this is to draw on Robert Ardrey's description of motivation in the higher animals. (Ardrey was both a playwright and an anthropologist, so I figure he has just the right credentials.) He theorized that all human beings seek

Security, Identity and Stimulation

which he defined by their opposites: anxiety, anonymity and boredom. We all seek these three things (assuming human beings can be included in the "higher animals" category) though not necessarily in equal proportions. While these three "needs" are not mutually exclusive, Ardrey felt that we are all driven by one or the other as a priority. *Lethal Weapon*'s Martin Riggs is driven by stimulation. *As Good As It Gets*'s Melvin Udall is driven by security. *Sunset Boulevard*'s Norma Desmond is driven by identity. Thus, those of us who are driven by stimulation, might try to climb Mount Everest, sacrificing security. If security is paramount in our psychological makeup, we might prefer a nice, steady job, pension guaranteed, along with a hobby like stamp collecting.

Since a character's motivation—Riggs's need to exorcise the tragedy in his life by pushing the envelope of danger, Murtaugh's desire to live through his remaining assignments and retire to the bosom of his family—is paramount in defining him/her, you might start with those basics, then chose your specifics. Keep in mind that a character's needs will drive their actions, and their actions will drive your screenplay. A character that doesn't need *something* isn't going to be very interesting.

Twists

Nothing, but nothing, satisfies the quality of unpredictability better than a turn in the plot that the audience doesn't expect. Filmgoers are saturated in the predictable. We *expect* the hero in an action movie to vanquish his foes by the last reel. We know that the leading man and leading lady will end up together.

But whoever expected Susan Sarandon to fall to her death off the wing of *The Great Waldo Pepper*'s barnstormer? (William Goldman thinks that unexpected death of the girl killed the picture's chances. I think it was one of the really bold flourishes in screenwriting history.) If an actor has good billing, something in the back of the audience's mind says, *he's/she's going to make it.*

Here's a now-classic twist people are still arguing over. ("Did you know before that scene?")

```
She comes out then, dressed in a silk kimono. She
looks extraordinarily beautiful. He reaches out his
hand and grasps hers. He draws her towards him. He
begins to kiss her face and neck.

                    FERGUS
            Would he have minded?

She murmurs no. His hands slip the wrap down from
her shoulders.

CLOSE ON his hands, traveling down her neck, in the
darkness. Then the hands stop. He realizes
something is wrong.

The kimono falls to the floor gently, with a
whisper. The camera travels with it. We see that
she is a man.

Fergus sits there, frozen in the darkness, staring
at her.

                    DIL
            Jimmy?

Her hand reaches out to his face, which is rigid.

                    DIL
            You did know, didn't you?

Fergus says nothing.

                    DIL
            Oh God. 8
```

Twists aren't so easy, since they tend to come from unpredictable set-ups, and that goes against the genre grain. Examining the list of the ten largest grossing films of all time, we don't see any particularly great plot twists. The credits of *Jurassic Park* alone let you know that something is going wrong in this amusement park, and it does, and it does and it does, with as predictable regularity as a scandal in Washington. But they're well worth including if you can think of one.

Here's a neat twist from a proto-typical category—the climactic battle:

```
And Kyle rolls with the last of his strength,
raising the pipe bomb he has been cradling. He jams
it between two hydraulic cylinders just beneath the
cyborg's armored ribcage. Then rolls off the
catwalk. Terminator has an instant to react,
reaching for the bomb, before it EXPLODES.

Sarah is pitched forward by the blast and slides on
the floor. Slams up against one wall. A withering
spray of shrapnel strafes the walls around her.
Pieces of scrap metal clatter throughout the
factory, raining down.

C.U. - SARAH, very still. She winces and opens her
eyes. Slowly looks up.

POV - SARAH, as the smoke clears. The Terminator is
GONE. Unrecognizable clumps of BURNING DEBRIS lie
scattered about. Looking down through the grating
floor she sees Kyle's body. LOW ANGLE ON KYLE F.G.,
Sarah on catwalk above. Kyle's eyes are half-open.
Still. His face peaceful. ANGLE ON ONE OF THE FIRES
climbing some plastic tubing and triggering a
SPRINKLER HEAD. It begins to rain. C.U. - SARAH
sitting up as the water runs over her. She looks
down. Protruding from her right thigh is a TWISTED
PIECE OF METAL. Shrapnel. Part of the cyborg. She
pulls it out, grimacing. Her leg is broken.

It is a long time before she can gather the will to
move.

SARAH'S POV - She sees a WALL PHONE several yards
away, beyond the debris from the explosion. She
starts to crawl toward it. She passes A LARGE CLUMP
OF DEBRIS, F.G.
```

ANGLE ON DEBRIS (FX) as it rolls over suddenly! Now recognizable as the TERMINATOR'S HEAD AND ARMS, with half of the scattered torso trailing wires and twisted metal.

IT LUNGES FOR HER!

Sarah wants to scream this time, from the depths of her soul, but there is no scream, only a dry shivering sob.

The Terminator drags itself SCRAPING over the floor, steel fingers clutching.

Sarah is shaking and whimpering as she scrabbles away, crawling in agony.

ANGLE ON CONVEYOR BELT as Sarah flops from the catwalk onto the MOVING STRIP. She is carried into the intricate lattice of equipment. Sarah rolls off weakly before going under a set of sorting rollers.

ANGLE THROUGH MACHINERY - ON THE TERMINATOR (FX) as it crawls after her, dragging its body. It tracks her unerringly, EYES GLOWING. [9]

The last minute resurrection and renewed attack by a villain you were sure the hero had already vanquished is almost predictable, but with appropriate sound cues, it never fails.

After *Terminator* was a huge success, creator James Cameron had a dramatic problem. His star was the film's villain. (Nobody was going to the sequel to see Michael Biehn.) Bringing him back from the metal pulp we last saw him as wasn't a problem—the virtue of time travel scripts is that they can accommodate almost any kind of logic—but predictability was. *Terminator 2* threatened to be just another episode of the stocky Austrian robot vs. Linda Hamilton. Cameron solved it cleverly. *T2* sets up that both a cop and the Terminator are looking for John Connor, an authority-shy teenager. We already know from the first film what the Terminator has in mind—annihilation. As both characters suspensefully close in on John, we get the following:

THE COP scans the crowded arcade. Glimpses John, looking back as he moves around a row of machines. Starts toward him.

JOHN sees the cop homing in and starts walking fast. Looks back. THE COP is shoving through clots of kids. One of them is slammed to the floor. An eddy of outrage behind the cop as he gains speed. John breaks into a run. So does the cop. Kids scatter like ten-pins as the cop charges after John. John sprints through the arcade's back office and storerooms.

INT. SERVICE CORRIDOR

John emerges through a fire door into a long corridor which connects to the parking garage. He's running full out, when around the corner ahead of him comes...

TERMINATOR. Time stretches to nightmarish crawl as John tries to brake to a stop. Terminator reaches into the box of roses.

SLOW MOTION. The cold black steel of the SHOTGUN emerges as the box falls open, the roses spilling to the floor. TERMINATOR'S BOOT crushes the flowers as it moves forward.

JOHN, transfixed by terror, is trapped in the narrow featureless shooting gallery of the corridor. THE SHOTGUN COMES UP. Terminator expressionlessly strides forward. Jacks a round into the chamber, slow and fluid.

John looks behind him for a place to run. Sees the cop coming toward him, pulling his Beretta pistol. Incredibly, John realizes the cop is aiming his gun at him! John looks back at Terminator. He is staring into the black muzzle of the 10-gauge now. Aimed right at his head. He realizes he's screwed. Then something crazy happens...

TERMINATOR
Get down.

John instinctively ducks. Terminator pulls the
trigger. KABOOM!

THE COP catches the SHOTGUN'S BLAST square in the
chest just as he fires the pistol. The pistol's
shot goes wild.

TERMINATOR pumps another round into him. Then
another. And another. Advancing a step each time he
fires, he empties the shotgun into the cop, blowing
him backward down the corridor. The sound is
DEAFENING. Then silence.

THE COP lies still on his back.

Terminator is now standing right over John. They
both watch as the cop, incredibly, sits up unharmed
and gets to his feet. Terminator grabs John roughly
by his jacket. Clutches the kid to his chest then
spins around as the cop opens fire with the
Beretta.

The "cop", who not only isn't a cop, he clearly
isn't even human, pulls the trigger so fast it
almost seems like a machine-pistol.

ON TERMINATOR'S BACK, as the 9mm slugs slam into
it, punching bloody holes in the motorcycle jacket.

JOHN is bug-eyed with fear, but completely
unscratched. Terminator's body has blocked the
bullets.

The Beretta CLACKS empty. Terminator turns at the
sound. Shoves John behind a Coke machine. Drops the
empty shotgun. Starts walking toward the "cop". The
empty magazine clatters to the floor. The cop
inserts another one. Snaps back the slide.
Terminator still has twenty feet to go. He doesn't
break his purposeful stride.

```
The cop opens fire. Bullets rake Terminator's
chest. He doesn't even flinch. Ten feet to go. BLAM
BLAM BLAM BLAM! Neither the cop nor Terminator show
the slightest change in expression as the gun rips
Terminator's wardrobe to shreds.

CLACK. The pistol empties again. Terminator stops
two feet in front of the cop. The appraise each
other for a second.

We realize now that the cop is a Terminator too. We
don't know the details yet, but let's call him the
T-1000 (since that's what he is). A newer model
than the one we've come to know so well (the 800
Series "Arnold"). This guy's a prototype...and he's
got quite a few surprises. 10
```

And voila: Arnold Schwartzenegger, the villain, suddenly becomes our hero.

The same author has a nice, if much smaller, twist in another script. After a blistering scene between the male and female leads, whose relationship we don't know, is played out, the woman leaves and:

```
            BRIGMAN
    God, I hate that woman.

            CARNES
    You probably shouldn't have
    married her then. 11
```

And since we assumed they weren't married, that came as a nice twist.

Whammies

When in doubt have a man come through a door with a gun in his hand.
—Raymond Chandler

If old Broadway wisdom says that you shouldn't go too long in a musical without a musical number, then it's fair to say that you shouldn't go too long in an action film without action, or a comedy without gags. The modern film producer/executive calls the action sequence in an action film The Whammy. Naturally, they want a lot of them. One king of action films specifies one every ten pages.

The concept fits with all kinds of films, however. In a comedy, think of the whammy as a scene giving the lead comic the opportunity to slip on the banana peel, get a broom caught in his mouth, whatever. If you count the shootings in an Arnold Schwartenegger film, or the bits (shtick, or hunks, vaudeville used to call them) in a Jim Carrey film, you'll see that the modern movie is composed of as many of these as can be placed in the story. (Make that jammed in, and the story be damned.) The problem that the screenwriter faces is that producers expect to get a lot of bang for their buck. They want a whammy every few pages. The more, the merrier. Each must be larger and more spectacular than the last. *Terminator* is one of my favorite concepts. The leading man is a robot with extraordinary powers of self-rejuvenation, so you can blow his head off in the first whammy, and still have him around for even greater humiliation in the next. An ideal set-up for increasingly larger whammies.

Here's the first whammy in a good screenplay:

```
INT. HOLD

Kane approaches the center of the room.
On the floor are rows of leathery ovoid shapes.
He walks around them.
Shines his light on one.

                    KANE
          It's like some kind of
          storage area. Is anybody
          there? Do you read me?

                    DALLAS
               (voice over)
          Loud and clear.

                    KANE
          The place is full of
          leathery things
          sealed...soft to the touch.
```

                    DALLAS
                (voice over)
        Can you see what's in them?

                    KANE
            I'll give it a look.

He tries to open one of them.
It won't open.

                    KANE
        Strange feeling to it.

                    DALLAS
                (voice over)
        Don't open it. You don't
        know what's in it.

Kane peers closely at the leathery ovoids.
Turns away.
Raised areas begin to appear where he touched it.
He moves his light along the rows.
Turns back to the one he was examining.
Something has changed.
The opaque surface begins to clear.
Object becoming visible within.
Kane shines his light on the floor at the base of
it.
He studies it.

                    KANE
            Jesus...

                    DALLAS
                (voice over)
            What?

Viscera and mandible now visible.
The interior surface spongy and irregular.
Kane shines the light inside.
With shocking violence, a small creature smashes
outward.
Fixes itself to his mask.
Sizzling sound.

The creature melts through the mask.
Attaches itself to Kane's face.
Kane tears at the thing with his hands.
His mouth forced open.
He falls backward.

INT. CHAMBER ABOVE

          DALLAS
    Kane...Kane can you hear me?

Here's the second whammy in the same script:

INT. CORRIDOR OUTSIDE INFIRMARY WINDOW

What they see is...Not what they expect.
Kane is sitting up in bed...wide awake.
They enter...

         LAMBERT
    Kane...Are you all right?

         KANE
    Mouth's dry...can I have
    some water?

Instantly, Ash brings him a plastic cup and water.
Kane gulps it down in a swallow.

         KANE
    More.

Ripley quickly fills a much bigger container.
Hands it to Kane.
He greedily consumes the entire contents.
Then sags back, panting, on the bunk.

         DALLAS
    How do you feel?

         KANE
    Terrible. What happened to
    me?

                    ASH
You don't remember?

                    KANE
Don't remember anything. I
can barely remember my name.

                    PARKER
Do you hurt?

                    KANE
All over. Feel like
somebody's been beating me
with a stick for about six
years.
        (smiles)
God, I'm hungry.

                    RIPLEY
What's the last thing you
can remember?

                    KANE
I don't know.

                    DALLAS
Do you remember what
happened on the planet?

                    KANE
Just some horrible dream
about smothering. Where are
we?

                    RIPLEY
We're on our way home.

                    BRETT
Getting ready to go back
into the freezers.

                    KANE
I'm starving. I want some
food first.

                    PARKER
        I'm pretty hungry myself.

                    DALLAS
        One meal before bed.

INT. MESS

The entire crew is seated.
Hungrily swallowing huge portions of artificial
food.
The cat eats from a dish on the table.

                    KANE
        First thing I'm going to do
        when we get back is eat some
        decent food.

                    PARKER
        I've had worse than this,
        but I've had better too, if
        you know what I mean.

                    LAMBERT
        Christ, you're pounding down
        this stuff like there's no
        tomorrow.

Pause.

                    PARKER
        I mean I like it.

                    KANE
        No kidding.

                    PARKER
        Yeah. It grows on you.

                    KANE
        It should. You know what
        they make this stuff out
        of...

                    PARKER
          I know what they make it out
          of. So what. It's food now.
          You're eating it.

Suddenly Kane grimaces.

                    RIPLEY
          What's wrong.

Kane's voice strains.

                    LAMBERT
          What's the matter?

                    KANE
          I don't know...I'm getting
          cramps.

The others stare at him in alarm.
Suddenly he makes a loud groaning noise.
Clutches the edge of the table with his hands.
Knuckles whitening.

                    ASH
          Breathe deeply.

Kane screams.

                    KANE
          Oh God, it hurts so bad. It
          hurts. It hurts.
               (stands up)
          Ooooooh.

                    BRETT
          What is it? What hurts?

Kane's face screws into a mask of agony.
He falls back into his chair.

                    KANE
          Ohmygooaaaahh.

```
A red stain.
Then a smear of blood blossoms on his chest.
The fabric of his shirt is ripped apart.
A small head the size of a man's fist pushes out.
The crew shouts in panic.
Leap back from the table.
The cat spits, bolts away.
The tiny head lunges forward.
Comes spurting out of Kane's chest trailing a thick
body.
Splatters fluids and blood in its wake.
Lands in the middle of the dishes and food.
Wriggles away while the crew scatters.
Then the Alien being disappears from sight.
Kane lies slumped in his chair.
Very dead.
A huge hole in his chest.
The dishes are scattered.
Food covered with blood.
```

                    LAMBERT
        No, no, no, no, no. [12]

And that's only the first ten pages. The movie has barely started.

Many screenwriters who use the index-cards-on-the-bulletin board system to outline their story put their whammies on red cards. When they stand back, if there aren't enough red cards, they know something's wrong. We might extend that and suggest putting action sequences (or comic sequences in a comedy) on red cards, unexpected plot twists on green cards, and good character traits on yellow cards. When your bulletin board looks like a rainbow coalition, you're ready to advance to first draft.

Running through the script for a very successful sci-fi action film, I wrote down the following:

scene #
1 - meet protagonist
2 - meet antagonist - first whammy
17 - two whammies
- long suspenseful sequence -
60 - whammy, but false alarm (made you jump!)
62 - whammy, real thing

67 - whammy, false alarm
70 - whammy, real thing
71 - intro surprise character
88 - big whammy
90 - whammy
92 - whammy
95-106 - major whammy (long action sequence)
113 - whammy
126 - whammy
141-146 - major whammy
151-190 - helluva whammy (climactic action sequence)
191 - surprise resurrection of antagonist
192-200 - whamoroonie!

Considering that each whammy was something of a heart stopper—
with good character evocations and plot twists in between—that's
very good structure.

Here's the time scheme of a successful Jim Carrey comedy, where
gags and bits (one comedy ploy or take), hunks (a series of escalat-
ing bits), or routines (stretching one bit out and building upon it)
stands for the whammies. Although a few supporting characters
garnered laughs as well, I only recorded the protagonist's success.
Clearly Carrey generates plenty of his own guffaws, yet each of his
opportunities is set up in the script.

The Set-Up
00:02:02	establish running gag
00:06:30	bit
00:10:34	bit
00:14:32	bit
00:17:45	bit
00:19:19	final plot set-up

The Complications
00:19:59	bit
00:21:44	bit
00:22:15	bit
00:23:00 - 00:24:00	hunk
00:25:00	bit
00:26:40 - 00:30:59	hunk

00:32:20 - 00:33:15	hunk
00:33:17 - 00:34:00	hunk
00:35:00	bit
00:40:45	bit
00:41:55 - 00:42:36	string of bits
00:44:30	two bits
00:46:00	bit
00:46:43 - 00:49:21	routine
00:49:49	bit
00:51:34	bit
00:52:25	bit
00:53:38 - 00:54:55	hunk
00:55:44	bit
00:59:20	bit
01:00:00	bit
01:01:40	bit
01:02:29	bit
01:04:00	bit
01:04:50	bit
01:08:20	bit

The Resolution

01:12:18 - 00:15:44	routine

The Denouement

01:20:26	finish running gag

Here's a successful cops and robbers action picture (big money spec sale *and* commercially successful release).

scene #

1A - whammy
19A - whammy
44 - whammy
57 - whammy
75 - whammy
83 - whammy
95 - whammy

Seven action sequences in the first half of the picture! In the second half of the picture, we get three consecutive big whammie sequences (scenes 112—173), followed by the denouement, then wrapping up with a surprise whammy, and the final fade.

Structure. You can take it to the bank.

Okay, you've written a great screenplay, and sold it. Or maybe you've gotten an assignment. Now you are facing a process often referred to by writers as Hell, which executives think of as. . .

Part 3

DEVELOPMENT

. . . .
DEVELOPMENT
. . . .

The road of good intentions is paved with Hell.

—Spencer Ante

In screenwriting, like much of life itself, you had better enjoy the process, because the result is not always satisfying. Failure can be tough. And success is a bitch. Although even the most experienced screenwriters harbor the secret belief that as soon as they turn in their first draft, the studio will jump up and shout, 'Don't touch a thing, let's shoot it!" the reality is always—make that ALWAYS—the opposite.

"Development" is an amorphous and infinitely variable process in which an idea for a movie becomes, painstakingly slowly, a shooting script for a film. Shepherding the idea-outline-treatment-first draft-second draft-polish-re-write-director's draft-star's draft along the way is a team of suits known variously as Directors of Development, or Managers-Directors-Vice Presidents-Executive Vice Presidents-Senior Vice Presidents-Presidents-of Production—all known as Creative Executives. Today's executive has a degree from a business school, and strong relationships with A-list creative personnel because they have been their agents or attorneys.

You have to take their notes and make them work. These people aren't stupid. They simply aren't writers, dramatically speaking. They have smarts, but often little creative intuition. So listen carefully; you don't want to miss something that just might turn out to be worthwhile.

And the less experienced these people are, the greater the effect they have on the script, because it's the junior executives who prepare the project. The Presidents and CEOs simply hear the idea and say yes or no.

In an endeavor to please these people and move the screenplay along the process toward actually becoming a film, many inexperienced writers put in and take out of their script everything that is suggested to them. I could advise you that this isn't wise. I could remind you that you have the original concept firmly in your mind, and only you can judge what enhances and what muddies that concept. A terrific idea for a scene doesn't necessarily mean a terrific scene for your movie. I could quote the best thing ever said to me by a fellow writer when I was fighting with an editor over a book's structure: "If you're going to have a failure, at least let it be your failure." I could tell you to stick to your guns. But then you won't succeed as a screenwriter, because the development people are the ones with the power to see that your film gets made.

I could also advise you to pay attention and satisfy them, in order to get your film made. That advice, however, hardly jibes with what I have seen for myself first hand: During a ten year history of reading scripts, I have seen innumerable scripts hurt by the development process. In nine out of ten cases, the screenplay got worse before it got made. Granted, it once in a while got better, but in those cases it was solely due to a good director who had a concept all along, and simply stuck to it, nodding his head and smiling during story meetings, then going back to his office and doing exactly what he knew was right.

You can't win. You can only play the game. Here's how:

• True story: one writer sold her first script for a fortune, then was replaced with a more experienced writer (the process of development) who proceeded to ruin the script. Just before shooting, the original writer had to be called in to re-write the re-write, whereupon she put her screenplay back into place, and everyone was satisfied. And successful. Moral: **Don't burn your bridges.** If you're going to be stubborn about your work, fine, but don't show it. Act accommodating. The executives you meet with do this all day, so you can probably count on them not remembering too much of what they told you to do anyway. The trick is to make your next draft better, one way or another, then give them credit.

• **Don't argue.** Discuss. If you tell someone they are wrong, they won't judge your argument, they'll judge you. We are all little individual egos in a universal game of bumper cars. Only the most secure and receptive person can change his course due to a well-reasoned argument, and receptivity is not common among the tense, ambitious, ego-driven personalities who gravitate to the movie business.

• Nod your head and smile. Pursue the point. If you get lucky, it might lead you to a good idea. Ask questions, **don't defend your film**. You can always ask, "Okay, if the girl DOESN'T die on page thirty, how should we keep her in the story?" Try not to put them on the spot. Pursue their points enthusiastically, through to the end until you both know whether it's a good idea or not.

• As long as you're not going to argue obstinately, **don't rationalize your writing** either. This is a common fault, shared by stubborn screenwriters who don't listen to good advice. Art stands for itself, and what a reader gets from your pages is probably more accurate than what you had in mind. Maybe you weren't clear enough.

• **Don't use your own vocabulary**. Use the executive's. Listen to what he/she's saying and figure out what he/she really means. Any good director knows that every actor comes from a different school of acting, with its own obscure, specific, sub-culture of definitions. He doesn't try to change that actor's understanding of key words. Instead he learns them himself, and uses the actor's vocabulary to work with him. Do the same with executives. Answer their questions and discuss your screenplay on their terms. When in Rome, speak Italian, and you'll get better directions. This isn't a morally reprehensible act, but a way to enhance communication. Many films have floundered because the writer was working on one concept, the producer on another, and the director on a third.

• **Don't discuss casting**. Your idea for casting a role (a good actor) isn't theirs (a box office bonanza). Let your creation speak for itself. If they insist on playing the "who do you see in this?" game, give them a number of different examples. You might hit one they like. Another good way to avoid specifics is, "a young Elizabeth Taylor," or "a James Dean type."

• **Don't dress better than the executive**. Be the artist. They're movie executives because they want to rub shoulders with you.

• **Don't talk too much.** Let them lecture. Most of them love to express their opinions. After all, if they were recluses they'd be writers. Their life is meetings, and they chose it. Don't look at a story conference as the one opportunity you've had to talk to someone other than your computer, and go crazy. (Speak in short sentences. The executive is going to answer his phone every few minutes, and then say, "where were we?")

• Try to see it as their movie, because that's the way they see it. Even if they bought *your* completely unique spec screenplay, remember that, especially in the film business, possession is nine-tenths of the law.

• Always say yes if they ask you if you want something to drink. It makes them feel appreciated. They're immediately suspicious of writers who say, "no, thanks."

Now go ahead. Take a meeting.

A Few Final Thoughts

• In the second half of the twentieth century American moviegoers have been treated to *Alien, Aliens, Alien3, Alien Resurrection, Alien Abduction, Alien Agenda, Alien Blood, Alien Contamination, Alien Dead, Alien Encounters, Alien Escape, The Alien Factor, Alien from L.A., Alien Intruder, Alien Nation, Alien Predator, Alien Prey, Alien Private Eye, Alien Seed, Alien Souls, Alien Space Avenger, Alien Species, Alien Terminator, Alien Thunder, Alien Transformation, Alien Vows, Alien Warrior, Alien Within, Alien Zone, Breakfast of Aliens, Sex and the Single Alien, My Uncle the Alien* and *My Stepmother Is an Alien*. (If you've seen them all, you probably subscribe to *Alien Weekly*.)

Readers cover alien scripts once a week. Don't let that encourage you to write *Alien Meter Maid*. If the subject is hot, you can bet that all the studios have it covered. They already have several projects "in development" on the subject, and there won't be room for yours, no matter how much better it might be. **Don't write current fads.**

Unless you have a great idea. What executives love more than anything is spelled out by this recent press quote in *Variety* from a major studio executive: "We want something that has more of an original edge to it but still is exploitative in nature and commercially viable." That's execspeak for "the same, only different." Something they're comfortable with, that makes them feel safe—a popular genre, last year's hit—with enough of a twist to sell it to the audience again. Walk the halls of the executive suite, and you'll hear shouts like, "*Air Force One* on an aircraft carrier!" "*Cliffhanger* under water!" "*The Exorcist* meets *Poltergeist!*"

Yet it's almost axiomatic that the next hot genre is precisely what is cold this season, because what studio executives never learn is that what the audience really wants is something truly new. (If you're interested in film at all, you already know that every studio in town turned down *Star Wars* because sci-fi was out, so I won't belabor that old story.)

I once took the true story of a famous athlete to a studio executive, and she said that sports as a genre was verboten, because sports fans sit in front of their televisions and don't go to films. I pointed out that the Academy Award for Best Picture had just gone to *Chariots of Fire*, and that *Rocky IV* was in pre-production. Without blinking an eye, she said, "Oh, but they're not sports films." **Don't argue with an executive**. They have an answer for everything, carved in lucite.

• The number of "personally committed writers" working on screenplays that "mean a lot to them" can be counted in the thousands. Usually down at the unemployment office. You want to make a movie of *The Cherry Orchard*? As they say in executive suites, not here you won't.

• Someone said that Russian literature was a book in which people with unpronounceable names talk to each other for 300 pages, then someone's aunt dies. It's all very well for witty people to stand around and talk to each other for two hours—English audiences adore this kind of theatre, and Europeans love it in film—but American films tend *not to get made* unless they have a great story.

Why this comes up is because of the number of screenwriters who, when asked to pitch their story, say "A man and a woman are in a relationship that is not working, and she finds the courage to leave him and become a single mother again."

Great. But it's not a commercial movie. This is a commercial movie: "A man and a woman rob a bank. She has a crisis of conscience, and turns him in."

Studios don't want to know about character studies, which they find boring. They want to know about action, which they can sell to the masses.

But here's the irony. That's the same movie.

A good story—especially if it's unique—will sell. Good stories need people and people need character and motivations and relationships, so you can put all that in just as well. *Jaws* might very well be about a policeman whose loyalty is torn between his job and his conscience. He has beachcombers to protect, but the Chamber of Commerce doesn't want him blabbing to tourists that their only four-star restaurant is the tourists themselves. For me that conflict was the most interesting theme in *Jaws*. But the studio isn't going to make a picture about a guy wrestling with his conscience. It's going to make a picture about a big fish that eats people.

• Experience is the best teacher. If you want to write—write. Pages every day. Make the time. Analyze your own work, making each attempt a little better.

• I've tried to use a number of short examples in this book, but there is no substitute for reading screenplays. Preferably for films that haven't been made yet, or at least films you haven't seen, so your impression is unsullied by the actual film. Avoid published screenplays. They are a transcription of the complete film, not the script, no matter how genuine they look. If you want to see how a screenwriter wrote a famous scene, go to the Writer's Guild Library (7000 West Third, Los Angeles, CA) or the Academy of Motion Pictures Arts and Sciences Library (333 South La Cienega, Los Angeles, CA), where you can reference the real thing.

•　　•　　•

You've thought of a story you are positive is next year's hot topic. You're going to avoid overwriting. Every sentence is going to clearly delineate what you want the reader to see on the screen.

If you've followed Denny's Don'ts closely, you'll be able to avoid an inept and amateur screenplay that the reader will put down within ten pages. You'll have a smooth read, and your story will plow forward with good pace.

That isn't quite enough. As I said in the beginning, I can't teach you to write well. No one can do that, although with a lot of practice, self and outside criticism, and stick-to-itiveness you'll get better and better. Writing is more like practicing the piano than people think. Talent is subjective, but hard work isn't. Woody Allen says 80 percent of success is showing up.

But if you want to write really well you need, in addition to born talent and acquired skill, a voice. A POV. You can tell a Gershwin tune whether or not you've heard it before. Don't underestimate the value of a personal style, as long as it doesn't directly counter the basic rules—without good reason. These rules aren't carved in stone. They're guideposts to keep you on track. (But **don't mix your metaphors.**)

Express yourself. No one else will. Good luck. And remember. . .

<pre>
            JOE
    Audiences don't know
    somebody sits down and
    writes a picture; they think
    the actors make it up as
    they go along. [1]
</pre>

APPENDIX

"Best" lists are subjective, unmanageable, opinionated, and inde-
fensible, but if you haven't seen these films, you probably should.
They're divided by genre, gleaned from everybody's favorites, and
limited to films in which the screenplay is well worth studying.

Dawn of an Art Form
Birth of a Nation
City Lights
Greed
M
Metropolis

Mystery/Thriller/Heist
And Then There Were None
Charade
The Conversation
The 39 Steps (1935)
The Lady Vanishes (1938)
The Maltese Falcon
The Parallax View
Rififi
The Third Man
Topkapi

Action/Adventure
The Bridge on the River Kwai
The Dirty Dozen
Treasure of the Sierra Madre
The Magnificent Seven

Noir
The Big Sleep (1946)
Body Heat
Chinatown
Double Indemnity
Out of the Past
Sunset Boulevard
Touch of Evil

Biography/Political
All the President's Men
Citizen Kane
Lawrence of Arabia
The Manchurian Candidate
Mr. Smith Goes to Washington
Patton
Sweet Smell of Success
Yankee Doodle Dandy

Sci-Fi
2001: A Space Odyssey
Charly
The Day the Earth Caught Fire
The Day the Earth Stood Still

Western

Bad Day at Black Rock
Butch Cassidy and the
  Sundance Kid
High Noon
Red River
Shane
The Searchers
Stagecoach (1939)
Unforgiven (1992)
The Wild Bunch

Gangster

Bonnie and Clyde
The Godfather (parts I & II
  cut together for Coppola's
  "Epic" edition)
Little Caesar
Miller's Crossing
Pulp Fiction
White Heat

Romance

The Best Years of Our Lives
Brief Encounter
Casablanca
Love in the Afternoon
Now, Voyager

Foreign Language

Beauty and the Beast (Jean
  Cocteau)
Children of Paradise
Jules and Jim
La Ronde (Max Ophuls)
The Seven Samurai

Horror

Invasion of the Body Snatchers
  (1956)
Psycho (1960)

Comedy

All About Eve
Duck Soup
Dr. Strangelove, or, How I
  Learned to Stop Worrying
  and Love the Bomb
The Graduate
It's a Wonderful Life
Kind Hearts and Coronets
M*A*S*H
Network
Some Like It Hot

Drama

The African Queen
The Deer Hunter
In a Lonely Place
On the Waterfront
Raging Bull

Musicals

42nd Street
7 Brides for 7 Brothers
An American in Paris
Cabaret
Gigi
Singin' in the Rain
Top Hat

ENDNOTES

Part 1—Form

[1] *Becket*, screenplay by Edward Anhalt, from the play by Jean Anouilh.

[2] *The Third Man* by Graham Greene.

[3] *Blade Runner* by Hampton Fancher and David Webb Peoples, from the novel *Do Androids Dream of Electric Sheep?* by Philip K. Dick.

[4] *Alien*, screenplay by Dan O'Bannon, story by Ronald Shusett and Dan O'Bannon.

[5] *Seinfeld*, "The Contest" by Larry David.

[6] *The Maltese Falcon*, screenplay by John Huston, from the novel by Dashiell Hammett.

[7] *The French Connection*, screenplay by Ernest Tidyman, from the novel by Robin Moore.

[8] *Robocop*, written by Michael Miner & Edward Neumeier.

[9] *When Harry Met Sally*, written by Nora Ephron.

[10] *Indiana Jones and the Last Crusade*, screenplay by Jeff Boam, story by George Lucas and Menno Meyjes.

[11] *The Rock* , shooting script by Jonathan Hensleigh.

[12] *Romancing the Stone*, written by Diane Thomas.

[13] *Raiders of the Lost Ark*, screenplay by Lawrence Kasdan, story by George Lucas.

[14] *The Adventures of Buckaroo Banzai Across the Eighth Dimension* by Earl Mac Rauch.

[15] *THX 1138*, written by George Lucas & Walter Murch.

[16] *Terminator*, written by James Cameron, Gale Ann Hurd, William Wisher Jr., acknowledgment: Harlan Ellison.

[17] *Sunday Bloody Sunday*, written by Penelope Gilliatt.

[18] *Aliens*, written by James Cameron.

[19] *Independence Day*, written by Dean Devlin & Roland Emmerich.

[20] *Dr. Strangelove, or, How I Learned To Stop Worrying and Love the Bomb*, written by Stanley Kubrick, Terry Southern, Peter George.

[21] *The Adventures of Buckaroo Banzai Across the Eighth Dimension*, written by Earl Mac Rauch.

[22] *The Graduate*, screenplay by Buck Henry and Calder Willingham, from the novel by Charles Webb.

[23] *When Harry Met Sally*, written by Nora Ephron.

[24] *Annie Hall*, written by Woody Allen and Marshall Brickman.

[25] *Dr. Strangelove, or, How I Learned To Stop Worrying and Love the Bomb*, written by Stanley Kubrick, Terry Southern, Peter George.

[26] *Aliens*, written by James Cameron.

[27] *The Elephant Man*, screenplay by Eric Bergen, Christopher DeVore & David Lynch, based on books by Ashley Montagu and Frederick Treves.

[28] *Aliens*, written by James Cameron.

[29] *Fargo*, written by Ethan Coen and Joel Coen.

[30] *Highlander*, written by Peter Bellwood, Larry Ferguson, Gregory Widen.

[31] *The Usual Suspects*, written by Christopher McQuarrie.

[32] *Raiders of the Lost Ark*, screenplay by Lawrence Kasdan, story by George Lucas.

[33] *Predator*, written by Jim Thomas & John Thomas.

[34] *Time After Time*, written by Nicholas Meyer.

[35] *Don Q*, unproduced, written by Nicholas Meyer.

[36] *Terminator*, written by James Cameron, Gale Ann Hurd, William Wisher Jr., acknowledgement: Harlan Ellison.

[37] *Casablanca*, screenplay by Julius J. Epstein, Philip G. Epstein & Howard Koch, from the play *Everybody Goes to Rick's* by Murray Burnett and Joan Alison.

[38] *Unforgiven* by David Webb Peoples.

[39] *Highlander*, written by Peter Bellwood, Larry Ferguson, Gregory Widen.

[40] *Braveheart*, written by Randall Wallace.

[41] *Die Hard*, screenplay by Jeb Stuart and Steven E. De Souza, from the novel *Nothing Lasts Forever* by Roderick Thorp.

[42] *The Rock*, shooting script by Jonathan Hensleigh.

[43] *The Abyss*, written by James Cameron.

Part 2–Content

[1] *Aliens vs. Predator*, unproduced screenplay by Peter Briggs.

[2] *Total Recall*, screenplay by Ronald Shusett & Dan O'Bannon and Gary Goldman, screen story by Ronald Shusett & Dan O'Bannon and Jon Povill, inspired by the short story, "We Can Remember It for You Wholesale" by Philip K. Dick.

[3] *The Rock*, shooting script by Jonathan Hensleigh.

[4] *The Hustler*, screenplay by Sidney Carroll and Robert Rossen, from the novel by Walter Tevis.

[5] *White Heat* story by Virginia Kellogg, screenplay by Ivan Goff, Ben Roberts.

[6] *Little Giants*, story by James Ferguson, Michael Goldberg, screenplay by James Ferguson, Michael Goldberg, Robert Shallcross, Tommy Swerdlow.

[7] *Lethal Weapon*, written by Shane Black.

[8] *The Crying Game*, written by Neil Jordan.

[9] *Terminator*, written by James Cameron, Gale Ann Hurd, William Wisher Jr., acknowledgment: Harlan Ellison.

[10] *Terminator 2: Judgment Day*, written by James Cameron and William Wisher Jr.

[11] *The Abyss*, written by James Cameron.

[12] *Alien*, screenplay by Dan O'Bannon, story by Ronald Shusett & Dan O'Bannon.

Part 3–Development

[1] *Sunset Boulevard.*, written by Charles Brackett, D.M. Marshman Jr., Billy Wilder.

OTHER FILM & ENTERTAINMENT BOOKS FROM LONE EAGLE PUBLISHING. . .

▰ SCREENWRITING ▰

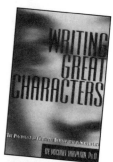

OTHER FILM & ENTERTAINMENT BOOKS FROM LONE EAGLE PUBLISHING. . .

 PRODUCTION

FILM PRODUCTION: THE COMPLETE *UNCENSORED* GUIDE TO INDEPENDENT FILMMAKING
by Greg Merritt

Too much of what passes for movie-making instruction is either an empty pep talk or a collection of impractical generalities. This book cuts through the fluff and provides the reader with real-world facts about producing and selling a low-budget motion picture ($500,000 and under). The book covers the complete management of a production from pre-production to principal photography to post-production through distribution. Includes chapters on Raising Money, Scheduling and Budgeting, Publicity and Festivals, Cast and Crew, Trouble Shooting, and Distribution.

$24.95 ISBN 0-943728-99-1, original trade paper, 6 x 9, 240 pp.

NEW EDITION...
THE FILM EDITING ROOM HANDBOOK
How to Manage the Near Chaos of the Cutting Room (3rd Ed.)
by Norman Hollyn

Editing is the creative force of filmic reality. Veteran Hollywood film editor Norman Hollyn has updated his well-written, semi-technical and profusely illustrated book. One of the most popular books used by film school instructors. The new chapters detail the procedural, creative and technical fundamentals of editing moving images within a computer-based, interactive environment, including an explanation of what nonlinear editing is, how it works, the creative flexibility it offers, and the time and cost savings it can achieve.

$24.95 ISBN 1-58065-006-6, original trade paper, 6 x 9, 448 pp, illustrated, bibliography, index.

BREAKING & ENTERING
Land Your First Job in Film Production
by April Fitzsimmons
Foreword by Gale Anne Hurd

An insider's guide to learning the ropes and gaining the proper tools and information to successfully enter into the fiercely competitive business of film production. This book is a great "A to Z" introduction for anyone who wants to get their feet wet in the entertainment industry. Full of hands-on information that pertains to day-to-day operations on the set during film or TV production . . . Real stuff, presented in a cool manner from an experienced pro.

$17.95 ISBN 0-943728-91-6, original trade paper, 6 x 9, 224 pp.

MOVIE PRODUCTION AND BUDGET FORMS...INSTANTLY!
by Ralph S. Singleton

Includes: Call Sheet, Production Report, Breakdown Sheets, Deal Memos, 84-page Feature Budget Form, and more. This book plus one photocopy machine equals every production and budget form needed to make a full-length feature or tele-film. Completely re-designed and integrated forms that are 8.5" x 11" format, ready to tear out and use over and over again.

$19.95 ISBN 0-943728-14-2, original trade paper, 9 x 12, 132 pp.

To order or for more information,
call 1-800-FILMBKS (345-6257) or go to www.loneeagle.com

OTHER FILM & ENTERTAINMENT BOOKS FROM LONE EAGLE PUBLISHING. . .

▉ PRODUCTION ▉

FILM SCHEDULING
Or, How Long Will It Take To Shoot Your Movie? (Second Edition)
by Ralph S. Singleton

"Detailing step-by-step how one creates a production board, shot-by-shot, day-by-day, set-by-set to turn a shooting schedule into a workable production schedule...For every film production student and most professionals."
— Los Angeles Times

FILM SCHEDULING contains a new section on computerized film scheduling. This section not only analyzes and compares the various computer programs which are currently on the market but also instructs the reader on how to maintain personal control over the schedule while taking advantage of the incredible speed a computer offers.

$22.95 ISBN 0-943728-39-8. original trade paper, 6 x 9, 240 pp.

Used by ALL leading film schools

FILM BUDGETING
Or, How Much Will It Cost to Shoot Your Movie?
by Ralph S. Singleton

The companion book to the best-selling *Film Scheduling* and its workbook (*The Film Scheduling/Film Budgeting Workbook*), FILM BUDGETING takes the reader through the steps of converting a motion picture schedule to a professional motion picture budget.

Using Francis Coppola's Academy Award nominated screenplay, *The Conversation,* as the basis for the examples, Singleton explains the philosophy as well as the mechanics behind motion picture budgeting. Readers do not have to be computer-literate to use this text, although computer budgeting is discussed.

Included are a complete motion picture budget to *The Conversation,* footnotes, glossary and index. When used in conjunction with its companion workbook, *The Film Scheduling/Film Budgeting Workbook*, FILM BUDGETING can comprise a do-it-yourself course on motion picture budgeting.

$22.95 ISBN 0-943728-65-7, original trade paper, 6 x 9, 300 pp, illustrated.

RALPH S. SINGLETON produced *SUPER NOVA, MURDER AT 1600, LAST MAN STANDING, CLEAR AND PRESENT DANGER, LEAP OF FAITH,* and *ANOTHER 48 HRS.* He also won an Emmy award for producing the critically acclaimed television series, *Cagney & Lacey.* Former head of production for Francis Coppola's Zoetrope Studios, Singleton has earned his reputation as "one of the best in the business."

FILM SCHEDULING/ FILM BUDGETING WORKBOOK
Do-It-Yourself Guide
by Ralph S. Singleton

Complete DO-IT-YOURSELF workbook companion to *Film Scheduling* and *Film Budgeting.* Contains the entire screenplay to Francis Coppola's Academy Award nominated screenplay, *The Conversation,* as well as sample production and budget forms to be completed by the reader. All sheets perforated.

$19.95 ISBN 0-943728-07-X, original trade paper, 9 x 11, 296 pp.

To order or for more information, call 1-800-FILMBKS (345-6257) or go to www.loneeagle.com

OTHER FILM & ENTERTAINMENT BOOKS
FROM LONE EAGLE PUBLISHING. . .

◼ DIRECTING ◼

FILM DIRECTING:
KILLER STYLE & CUTTING EDGE TECHNIQUE
by Renee Harmon

This book is written for the director who, though skilled in basic directing techniques, wants advice on achieving the emotional and visual impact demanded by today's motion picture industry. Renee Harmon explores the relationship of the director with the star, producer, writer, production manager, editor, composer and all the major film craft professionals. Includes straight-from-the-hip advice, helpful hints, plus important do's and don'ts of filmmaking.

RENEE HARMON, PH.D., is the author of eight best-selling and critically acclaimed books on various aspects of the film business.

$22.95 ISBN 0-943728-91-6, original trade paper, 6 x 9, 224 pp.

◼ ACTING ◼

MAKING MONEY IN VOICE-OVERS
Winning Strategies to a Successful Career in TV, Commercials, Radio and Animation
by Terri Apple
Foreword by Gary Owens

This book helps the actor, radio DJ, vocal impressionist and amateur cartoon voice succeed in voice-overs, no matter where you live. From assessing one's competitive advantages to creating a demo tape to handling initial sessions, Apple provides a clear guide full of insider tips and strategies helpful to both beginners and experienced professionals.

TERRI APPLE is one of the top paid, award-winning voice-over actresses whose work is heard everyday all across the country. She lives in Los Angeles, California.

$16.95 ISBN 1-58065-011-2, original trade paper, 5.5 x 8.5, 224 pp.

NEXT!
An Actor's Guide to Auditioning
by Ellie Kanner and Paul G. Bens, Jr.

Written by two of Hollywood's hottest casting directors, NEXT! is the definitive insider's guide to successfully navigating the complicated maze of auditions and landing that all-important role in a movie or TV show. NEXT! details the common errors that most inexperienced actors make when auditioning.

ELLIE KANNER cast the TV pilot of *Friends* and *The Drew Carey Show*. **PAUL G. BENS, JR.** is a partner in Melton/Bens Casting.

$19.95 ISBN 0-943728-71-1, original trade paper, 7 x 9, 184 pp.

YOUR KID OUGHT TO BE IN PICTURES
A How-To Guide for Would-Be Child Actors and Their Parents
by Kelly Ford Kidwell and Ruth Devorin

Written by a top talent agent and a stage mom with three children working in film, TV and commercials, YOUR KID OUGHT TO BE IN PICTURES explains what the odds of success are, how to secure an agent, where to go for professional photographs, the auditioning process, lots of photographs, plus much more.

$16.95 ISBN 0-943728-90-8, original trade paper, 9 x 6, 280 pp.

To order or for more information,
call 1-800-FILMBKS (345-6257) or go to www.loneeagle.com

ABOUT THE AUTHOR

Denny Martin Flinn grew up in San Francisco and Los Angeles, fell in love with the theatre when he was taken as a child to see a road company of a big Broadway musical, majored in theatre arts at San Francisco State College, then traveled to New York, where for nearly two decades he worked as a dancer, choreographer and director in musicals. Turning to writing, his first book was *What They Did For Love*, the story of the making of the Broadway musical *A Chorus Line*. He followed that with two mystery novels—*San Francisco Kills* and *Killer Finish*—featuring the grandson of Sherlock Holmes. Moving to Hollywood, he began at Paramount Pictures as a temp and worked his way down to screenwriting. With Nicholas Meyer he co-authored the screenplay for *Star Trek VI: The Undiscovered Country*, and two radio plays for the BBC: *Don Quixote*, and an adaptation of Meyer's novel *The Seven-Per-Cent Solution*. Several solo screenplay assignments followed. He is the author of the Star Trek novel *The Fearful Summons* (Star Trek #79) and *Musical! A Grand Tour—the Rise, Glory and Fall of an American Institution*. He currently lives in Los Angeles with his wife, their two children, and a dog who is writing a screenplay.